Exercise
and the
Mind

Paul Kiell, a psychiatrist living in Far Hills, New Jersey, has participated in marathon running and long-distance swimming, and has written extensively on both. He is the author of the biography of the great Glenn Cunningham, *American Miler*.

Exercise and the Mind

THE POSSIBILITIES FOR
MIND-BODY-SPIRIT UNITY

Paul J. Kiell, M.D.

BREAKAWAY BOOKS
HALCOTTSVILLE, NEW YORK
2010

Published by Breakaway Books
P.O. Box 24
Halcottsville, NY 12438
www.breakawaybooks.com

10 9 8 7 6 5 4 3 2

CONTENTS

AUTHOR'S NOTE

My quest is to demonstrate how the exercise habits of philosophers, poets, musicians, artists, writers, and statesmen affected their minds and their work.

The first chapter will define exercise within the context of this book. It will be an exercise prescription.

Next I describe Highland Hospital, founded in 1904 by Dr. Robert S. Carroll (1869-1949), a psychiatrist. There, in Asheville, North Carolina, the treatment for psychiatric patients focused on proper nutrition and vigorous exercise. In 1944 Highland Hospital was taken over by Duke University. Later scientific studies do show that Carroll's approach is effective, helping people burdened by mood disorders. Fittingly, the significant research is from Duke University, conducted by Dr. James Blumenthal, vindicating the thinking espoused by Dr. Carroll.

The next chapter tells of the explorer Meriwether Lewis, contrasting his state of mind when engaged in vigorous physical challenges with his behavior in sedentary life. Absent the physical challenges encountered in the expedition, he committed suicide. Here, in this chapter, the concept of the endorphins and the runner's high first enters.

Listening to music, too, can stimulate endorphins. Accordingly, the chapter to follow tells of composer Gustav Mahler and his exercise habits; of poet-philosopher Henry David Thoreau and his approach to exercise and the effect it had on his creativity—similar to the creativity of William Wordsworth and not unlike the problem-solving solutions exercise held for statesman, scientist, and soldier Jan Christian Smuts.

For Smuts, a vigorous exercise routine helped him to solve problems he "had in mind." The wellspring of the mind is the brain. Exercise, too, has a salutary effect in cases of injury to the brain. To illustrate the possible benefits in both brain injury and degenerative diseases of the brain, such as Alzheimer's, the case history of Trisha Meili, also known as the Central Park Jogger, now takes form.

In that presentation, scientific data supporting the beneficial role of exercise will be proffered, but there was one more element Meili brought into the arena, and that was her indomitable spirit. And so the chapters that follow will be about people I've met along the way who manifest those qualities we call "spirit."

When I say "along the way" I am speaking of people encountered during two decades of marathon running and nearly two decades of masters swimming competition. But none of my experience was in a vacuum, and it did not begin one day and end the next. Rather it begins from the beginning.

Many of the people who have helped me arrive at

this juncture, knowingly or otherwise, in ways great or small but always significant, come under the heading of family. For example, I am grateful to my now grown children, Susan, Charles, Ellen, Lisa and Amy, for allowing me to teach them and in doing so teaching me even more. So, too, my wife Benita, a perpetual fountain of support and encouragement. The source, however, for all of us resides with my late father, Dr. Isidor Kiell, who by his personal example conveyed an appreciation of sport, but always in proportion, always in perspective, always emphasizing its transcendent value and essence as a mirror and lesson for life itself.

How you comported yourself on the playing field would be a model for how you acted on the stage of life; the effort you put in to your physical activity would be a metaphor for the commitment you gave to your vocation, to your friends, to your family.

I include among family my dear friend, the late Dr. Ralph Paffenbarger. His contributions to the field of exercise and health have been legion. Holding chairs at the Stanford University School of Medicine and the Harvard Medical School, he was a pioneer in his 1970s study of the San Francisco longshoremen, with their exercise habits translated into Calories expended per week in their work. He correlated Caloric expenditure with incidence of heart disease and all-cause mortality. He was, furthermore in the forefront of the ongoing Harvard/ Stanford Alumni Study correlating physical activity with degrees of health, disease, and mortality.

All told, from all of the studies he led or participated in, he was able to demonstrate how degrees of exercise contribute to lowering risk of hypertension, heart attacks, stroke, peptic ulcer disease, diabetes, accidental death, suicide, cancer, and "other distresses of middle and later ages." He found, too, that when people begin regimens of vigorous physical exercise in middle or even later life, benefits still accrue to them.

Precise and always mindful of scientific validity, he once wrote me that to some degree, we still lack data to indicate what kinds, how much, and how intense exercise should be to promote optimal health. Nevertheless, in his two-decade study of energy expenditure in San Francisco longshoremen, he did calculate the value of Caloric expenditure equivalent to about twenty miles a week of jogging, brisk walking, or running, in lowering the risk of heart disease.

Based on the evidence he gleaned, Ralph demonstrated that exercise, in the right intensity and dosage, clearly enhances the oxygen-carrying capacity of the cardiovascular system. Fitness of the cardiovascular system, as will be demonstrated in this book, correlates in a decidedly positive fashion with intellectual and emotional health. We remember from high school geometry: that things equal to the same thing are equal to each other; so, too, does fit body equal fit mind. That truth was initially enunciated in the first century by the Roman poet Juvenal: "Our prayers should be for a sane mind in a healthy body (*mens sana in corpore sano*)."

Despite authoring over 150 scientific papers and running in almost the same number of marathons and ultramarathons, Paffenbarger still felt that he had failed to get his message across. He was neither "popularizer" nor cheerleader; his modest self-effacing style precluded any such push. Courtly in manner, dull and boring in his nuance-ridden scientific explanations, he was neither evangelical nor charismatic.

His constant lament centered on the question, "How are we going to get more people to exercise?" Ralph insisted that whatever you preached or wrote about must be scientifically valid. Hoping that I won't have strayed from his strict ethic, I most humbly dedicate this work to the memory and work of Dr. Ralph S. Paffenbarger. Hopefully, too, the material and approach here will be one small step toward fulfilling Ralph's dream of getting more people to engage in vigorous exercise as a way of life.

Paul J. Kiell, M.D.
Far Hills, New Jersey, 2010

FOREWORD

Patrick J Hogan, D.O.

Exercise and the Mind points to the direct benefits of physical exercise for promoting brain health. *Exercise and the Mind* brings the science of exercise to life as it captivates us with the personal stories of historic figures reaping the benefits of physical exercise on the brain.

Dr. Paul Kiell has been able to merge his longtime personal experience of endurance exercise with his psychiatric insight into human nature, thus formulating a greater understanding of how our lifestyle choices can improve the very health and attitude of our minds. He combines this with examples of the indomitable human spirit.

Gone are the days that we relegate the benefits of exercise only to the muscles and heart. We now recognize that by challenging the muscular system there springs forth a mighty feedback mechanism that nourishes the very structure and chemical balance of the brain. "Exercising the muscles is exercising the brain" becomes our new life maxim. In fact, the beneficial adaptive response to challenging exercise arises consequent to direction from the brain itself.

People had assumed that the benefits to the brain from exercise were related to increased blood flow and oxygen. The brain was thought to be a rigid organ born with as many cells (neurons) as it would have in life, and that these neurons would be slowly lost over the years. As it turns out, our brains are more moldable (plastic) in response to the right stimulus. We now know that there is a dynamic interplay between the body and the brain occurring during exercise that activates the release of otherwise dormant brain chemicals that, in turn, produce formation of new neurons and connections (synapses). As a result of this phenomenal process, the functions of our brain can improve any time through all stages of life. Furthermore, brain diseases and aging effects that were once felt inevitable can be forestalled or prevented.

What is equally important is the special ability of exercise to enhance the neurotransmitters in the brain in just the right way. We depend on the proper balance of the chemical soup in our brains to modulate our mood, shape our attitudes for life, and maintain proper interactions with other people. When this chemical balance is disturbed, medications are often necessary to help reestablish control of the mind.

Exercise has the distinct advantage of bringing the soup of the brain chemicals into just the right mix and sustaining it better than is possible with antidepressant medications alone. This is demonstrated in the lives of historical figures outlined here in *Exercise and the Mind* who became benefactors of exercise as the best medicine.

There is always the question of how much and what type of exercise is needed for this medicine to do its greatest good. In the first chapter, there is a guideline for anyone to follow to develop a personal exercise program. It is a matter of finding the pattern that fits the individual so that exercise becomes an everyday life style. As Dr. Kiell emphasizes, the key is to challenge the brain through exercise in a diversified and, yes, a playful manner. Such can be done through a mix of strength training, core training such as Pilates, and mobility training such as yoga and aerobic training, in such a manner that your brain perceives it as challenging. A total mix of exercise forms is ideal.

Too often, however, people are adhering to the idea of exercise with a level of exertion that is too casual, or at best tedious and boring. Although our brains must recognize the exercise to be moderately difficult at first for the adaptive changes of brain and body to come about, exercising should not be painful, boring, or overly tedious, or anything like taking bitter medicine. Rather it should be enjoyable, if not even actually exhilarating. We were meant to be active. Exercise mobilizes our body for the test ahead. Given the challenge of physical activity our resources are mobilized; we are mentally keener; our hearts beat more efficiently; neurohormones designed to elevate our mood and fine-tune our thinking are activated. We become the best we can be.

Truly, exercise is in itself a medicine, delivering dividends far exceeding anything Wall Street ever imagined.

So enjoy your reading of *Exercise and the Mind*. Learn how exercise stabilizes the functions of the human body. You will be inspired to create a personal exercise program and with it, the life and health of your body and mind.

Tacoma-based neurologist Patrick Hogan is director of the Puget Sound Regional Movement and Motility Disorder Clinic. There he works extensively with Parkinson's patients and people who suffer from dystonia, a neurological disorder characterized by involuntary, debilitating muscle contractions. Ever trumpeting his message that exercise is medicine, he has started Dance for Parkinson programs and the first Dance for Dystonia program in the country.

PRESCRIPTIONS

Since the benefits of vigorous exercise, particularly as it affects the mind, will be discussed here, it is wise to define what I'm talking about when I say "exercise."

A photo of the German Olympic Women's Gymnastic Team at the 1928 Olympiad. Very likely this photo was the inspiration for the classic beach running scene in *Chariots of Fire*.

Most critical: Whatever the choice of exercise, it should be playful and fun. Dr. George Sheehan put it this way: "Find the boy in the man and then the dream in the boy and that is what your play is." Another example: using basketball as his metaphor, Pat Conroy in the prologue of his book *My Losing Season*, wrote how the sport allowed him glimpses into the kind of man he was capable of becoming. Once he got into the flow and rhythm of the game, "I was the happiest boy who ever lived."

The play, too, should be suited to the player. I'll illustrate with the example I know best, myself. I was a competitive swimmer and occasional competitive runner in both high school and college. Then, from age twenty-two to about thirty-eight, the demands of school, vocation, and family shifted my attention and energies away from engaging in any form of exercise, save a once-a-week round of golf when the weather allowed. Then I began taking long walks in the woods just across the street with my Labrador retrievers.

It could have begun and ended with long walks. Walking is ideal. The woods provided a quiet natural escape. It was a form of play, one with rhythm, scenery, and peace. But there was always the dream, the dream to run a marathon. So I began jogging, then running longer distances, later finding camaraderie in new friends with like strivings.

Twenty years, fifty-two marathons and ultramarathons later, having had bestowed upon me a serious injury, I returned to swimming. Both running and swimming have the advantage of using large-muscle groups and can be done in solitude or with company. I was competitive only because it was right for me, but it's not necessarily required of anyone else. Yet it let me be a kid again, enjoying the fellowship of guys and girls of all ages doing the same thing.

Swimming, artistically next to dance, comes closest to music with its rhythms and emphasis on meticulous technique. Dancing too—specifically aerobic dancing—may be best for some. For example, the Zumba Fitness Program combines Latin rhythms with continuous aerobic exercise involving all of the muscle groups.

For many, dancing is ideal. Particularly plain old ballroom dancing. To quote Dr. Hogan, who kindly penned this book's foreword: "Nothing engages balance, complex lateral movement, rhythm, cognitive processes, social skills, and vigorous aerobics quite like ballroom dancing." The implication for management of various disorders of the central nervous systemsuch as Parkinson's or even some of the dementias like Alzheimer's, is intriguing.

Just as music is basic and universal, so, too, is one of its by-products, dance. Accordingly, it is wise to spend a little more time describing its potential, particularly since it requires little or no equipment and can be done anywhere. To again quote Dr. Hogan:

> A program of dance on a regular basis provides an ideal means of enhancing the exercise routine. People often deny themselves the benefits of dance because of self-doubts of their ability or rhythm. Dance, however, has been discovered to be part of the basic human experience for mil-

lenniums. Everyone has innate rhythm as demonstrated by watching a toddler dancing to music or by rhythmical activities we do in daily life.

Dance training has been demonstrated in research to stimulate more networks in the brain than any other exercise due to the nature of what the brain has to do in order to dance with a partner, to dance in rhythm to music, and to dance with specific dance steps. Dance has specifically been researched to control depression. More than other exercise, dance has been extensively studied in Parkinson's disease to improve mobility, balance and mood.

It is a matter of making exercise fun and varied so that it carries you to greater health and happiness throughout your life.

Bicycling, jogging or running, cross-country skiing, and kayaking—any of these or any mixture may be the best choice. Akin to dance, with practice, they can be done rhythmically, bringing with them an element of meditation. In fact, best of all is where there are combinations of all types of exercise regimens.

How long, how much? As long as you are still enjoying it, avoiding boredom, and avoiding—rather eschewing—the concept that there is no gain without pain, you will find your own limits.

Should you be gasping for air? No! Run, walk or jog, swim or paddle or ski or dance at a pace where you can still talk to a companion or yourself. The "talk test" is an important guide, reminiscent of philosopher-physician Maimonides who, a thousand years ago, told us to exercise "to the point of breathlessness."

Henry David Thoreau, about whom you'll read in a later chapter, had much to say about life and really about exercise, telling us that we should move to the beat of our own drummer. He cautioned against overdoing exercise and trying to reach lofty goals too soon. "Shall he turn his spring into summer," he wrote, "we shall not be shipwrecked on a vain reality." *Shipwrecked* translates to injury, the bane of the dedicated exerciser.

Duration of effort to earn health benefits begins roughly at thirty minutes of effort, but with the caution that every other day should be a bit easier than the one just before, that is, it's best to alternate hard and easy days—with maybe a day or two of rest each week. The 30-minute goal need not be reached in one effort; it can be two or more exertions over the course of the day. More than 30 minutes can easily be reached, but again the limiting factor depends on your goal. Like water, everyone will seek and find their personal level of activity. *Always:* Set goals that are a challenge, but are sensible, reasonable, and within reach.

Weight training, if you like it, involving frequent repetitions at lighter weights, is good. I was never one to stick to a program of body strengthening or even stretching, although the latter is a must. Stretching regimens definitely, fashioned after yoga principles and following an exercise bout while your muscles are still warm, are critical.

There are books, there are authorities, all too numerous to even think of listing. But if you follow simple basic fundamentals, you cannot go wrong and you will harvest abundantly. Help, again depending on goals, can be found at a local "Y" where at the same time there is group support and structured programs. Local informal running, skiing, swimming, kayak, and bicycling clubs are very helpful, especially if you want at some point to enter age-group competitions. There is an energy that flows from the camaraderie and support of like-minded souls.

Equipment and clothing should also be as simple as possible. Usually an army-navy store and a local running, ski, bicycle, or swim shop where you know the salespeople and have a rapport with someone knowledgeable is important. There, your needs as far as what shoes to wear, what bathing suit or goggles to buy, can be satisfied. You can skimp on most anything but running/walking shoes and goggles. For the shoes, stick for the most part to name brands.

Nutritional requirements, as complicated a subject as you may want to make it, still can be satisfied by making the meals balanced with as many fresh fruits and vegetables, whole grains and fiber as possible; as few refined sugars, additives, and saturated fats as possible; plus moderation in alcohol and total prohibition of smoking. Red meat is not necessarily forbidden, but should be eaten in moderation.

Vitamin supplementation is a subject still in transition. Given our environment (air pollution), it's probably wise to supplement with more antioxidants (Vitamins C and E) than has heretofore been thought. Scientific research has strongly hinted at increased needs for some vitamins, particularly vitamin D.

Weight loss and later weight stabilization are particularly apparent in running and cycling. Here the body temperature is raised so that there is an "afterglow" when you rest. While you are resting, that slight rise of temperature burns more Calories than if you did not run or cycle. Swimming, although it may consume an equivalent number of Calories to running, does not raise body temperature or heart rate enough to give that "afterglow." My experience is that it does not, of itself, encourage a weight loss, but does prevent weight gain.

Diets, if there are such things, are practically always products of quackery. Weight loss must be slow and gradual. It is a truism that the quicker the weight is lost, the faster it comes back the next time, with even more gain of fat. The longer and more gradual the weight loss, the longer it stays off. Weight management always, yes *always*, means joining exercise to sensible eating habits.

This workable prescription for exercise is part common sense and part science. Combined, it is not only a philosophy of exercise but also a metaphor, hopefully, for much of life itself.

ZELDA'S SANITARIUM

In his anthology titled *Runners and Other Ghosts on the Trail*, John L. Parker Jr. writes a short story he calls "For Amy on the Trail, Watching." In this tale, Parker has embarked on a solitary run. These lines tell us first where he is:

> These sad old mountains mesmerize . . . This is Cedar Mountain, North Carolina, within yelling distance of the Blue Ridge Mountains . . .

Then he gets to a certain spot:

> Thomas Wolfe strode these crags. And a long time ago they put crazy old Zelda Fitzgerald up in a rubber room at a place in Asheville. "I have lost my capacity to hope," F. Scott Fitzgerald wrote, "on the little road that led to 'Zelda's sanitarium.'"

"Zelda's sanitarium" was the Highland Hospital, perhaps the first modern systematic approach to treating disorders of the mind using the resources of exercise and nutrition. First known as "Dr. Carroll's Sanatorium," it was founded in 1904 by Dr. Robert S. Carroll (1869-1949), a distinguished psychiatrist. His

Dr. Carroll, second from right.

Highland Hall, circa 1943.

program of treatment for mental and nervous disorders and addictions was based on exercise, diet, and occupational therapy. Attracted to the natural surroundings and to the philosophy of the program, patients came from all over the country.

Dr. Carroll was ahead of his time. He advocated vigorous exercise such as a five-mile hike each day in Highland Park. He was strict on diet, too, ordering balanced regimens of wholesome foods. His ideas echoed the prescient thinking of the seventeenth-century poet John Dryden ("To My Honour'd Kinsman, John Driden"):

> Better to hunt in fields for health unbought,
> Than fee the doctor for a nauseous draught.
> The wise for cure on exercise depend;
> God never made his work for man to mend.

We'll never know if, or to what extent, Dr. Carroll's approach helped Zelda. Her clinical diagnoses ranged from schizophrenia to manic-depressive illness. She was depressed and probably alcoholic. She even showed later signs of dementia. At one time she had consulted with Sigmund Freud. There were many confounding

Highland Park circa 1943,
their hunting fields for health unbought.

variables in her life, including a tumultuous relationship with her alcoholic husband.

In 1944, Duke University assumed directorship of "Zelda's Sanitarium," the Highland Hospital. Four years later, on the night of March 10, 1948, a deadly fire broke out in the main building and took the lives of nine women, including Zelda Fitzgerald.

Fittingly, however, from that long-ago transfer of the Highland Hospital to Duke University, there is a tendril of connecting thread. It is research from Duke University that both bridges and vindicates Dr. Carroll's approach. Since the latter half of last century, although there has been a plethora of studies on exercise and mood disorders, this particular study, published in 1999, conducted by a Duke University team—in a sense, Dr. Carroll's progeny—was headed by psychologist Dr. James A. Blumenthal.

The Blumenthal group studied 150 participants suffering with mild to moderate degrees of major depressive disorder. The study would give some evidence, however incomplete, that exercise has a beneficial effect on the depressed population. The participants were randomly divided into three groups. One group was given an antidepressant medication (sertraline), another put on an exercise regimen (treadmill or stationary bicycle), and the third group was placed on a combination of exercise and antidepressant medication.

Beneficial outcomes from all three groups were reported along with some surprising results. But defects in the study were also self-reported.

After four months, all three groups had similar and significantly lower rates of depression. The surprising and hard-to-explain finding was that six months later, the group that merely exercised without receiving any medication had a significantly lower relapse rate compared with the medication group and the combination group.

Two issues now needed examination and clarification. One was the amount of exercise needed for a therapeutic effect. The other—the defect in their study—was a lack of controls. Without controls (no intervention) we never know whether the positive effects could be just a matter of the natural course of the illness or were the result of the therapeutic intervention.

How much exercise is needed to help depressed patients? There was a study of eighty adult patients ranging in age from twenty to forty-five and diagnosed with mild to moderate major depressive disorder (MDD). Here the participants were divided randomly into four exercise treatment groups and one control group. The exercise control group did flexibility exercises three times a week.

The four exercise treatment groups were divided according to quantity and frequency of exercise. Quantity was determined by Calories (kcal) expended; frequency was defined as exercising either three times a week or five times a week. Results were measured after twelve weeks.

The result was that after twelve weeks, scores on a standard test for depression were lowered 50 percent more for the higher-Caloric-expenditure patients as compared with both the lower-dosage patients and the controls. Frequency of exercising (three or five times a week) made no difference. The difference in results between the higher-Caloric-expenditure treatment group versus the control and the low-dosage exercise groups was statistically significant.

Back to Blumenthal: He later wanted to address the issue from his 1999 study of lack of controls. There were 202 patients diagnosed with major depressive disorder. The patients were randomly assigned to four different treatment conditions: a supervised exercise group, a home-based exercise group, an antidepressant medication group (fifty to two hundred milligrams of sertraline daily), a placebo for the control group. All groups were followed over a sixteen-week span. The Hamilton Depression Rating Scale and a clinical interview for depression were used to establish diagnosis.

After four months, the groups that exercised all showed statistically superior improvement compared with the controls.

(The authors from that particular study conclude with the usual disclaimer that further studies of exercise and its long-term benefits are needed. The feeling patients have of hope, the feeling that others care, combined with the eagerness to engage in treatment, must also be figured into the overall equation. Such is difficult to measure.)

Zelda Fitzgerald suffered from a mood disorder. The people treated in these studies usually are suffering with mild to moderate degrees of major depressive illness. These are people often functioning, despite illness—the so-called walking wounded. Some noteworthy historical figures from the past have been afflicted with mood disorders. One's well-being can fluctuate to polar degrees depending on levels of participation in vigorous exercise. The pursuit of vigorous exercise as compared with passive pursuit of the sedentary life played a pivotal role in the life of one particular historic figure, the American explorer of Northwest Passage fame, Meriwether Lewis.

NOTES:

Dementia refers to actual destruction of brain tissue from any cause, with characteristic signs of failure of memory, judgment, orientation and emotional control.

The Blumenthal group studied 150 participants . . . James A. Blumenthal, et al. Effects of exercise training on older patients with major depression. *Arch Intern Med* 1999; 159:2349-56.

Major depressive disorder refers to those patients feeling persistently sad, with loss of interest in activities and any combination of four additional symptoms: irritability, hopelessness, difficulty sleeping, low energy or fatigue, feelings of worthlessness or baseless guilt, appetite loss, difficulty concentrating, loss of feeling for favorite activities (anhedonia).

One group was given an antidepressant medication . . .
Antidepressants act by freeing up neurohormones from their
storage place in the nerve cells so that they can function in the
transmission of nerve impulses.

How much exercise is needed to help depressed patients?
Andrea L. Dunn, Madhukar H. Trivedi, James B. Kampert,
Camillia G. Clark, and Heather O. Chambliss, "Exercise treat-
ment for depression: Efficacy and dose response." *Am J Prev
Med* January 2005; 28(1):1-8

The four exercise treatment groups were divided . . .
To illustrate: In one group, a person weighing 150 pounds or
about 70 kilograms would be prescribed exercise expending 7
Calories per kilogram of body weight a week. In the other
group, 17.5 Calories per kilogram per week was prescribed.
The latter is *the* public-health-recommended dosage. In that
latter designation, it translates to about 1,225 Calories a week
expended in exercise that is above and beyond normal daily
activities. It also would be the equivalent of about 12 miles of
running, jogging, or brisk walking, or a little more than three
miles of swimming each week. The total weekly expenditure
could be performed in divided doses, that is, three times a
week or five times a week.

Quantity was determined by Calories (kcal) expended;
When we use the word calorie with lower-case c, we mean the
amount of heat to raise the temperature of one millimeter of
water one degree Celsius. But it is more accurate to refer to
kilocalories, or Calories using upper-case C. This refers to the
amount of heat needed to raise the temperature of one kilogram (about a quart) of water by one degree Celsius.

He later wanted to address . . . James A. Blumenthal, et
al., Exercise and pharmacotherapy in the treatment of major
depressive disorder, *Psychosom Med 2007;* 69:587-96.

control group: Scores/results on any experiment are compared from one group not receiving the treatment, for example, to the same scores in the experimental (treatment) group,
to counter the possibility that the experimental results could

not have otherwise come about spontaneously, over time, and without the experimental process (treatment). Control groups should be matched with the experimental group for age, gender, and other relevant characteristics.

The Hamilton Depression Rating Scale is a questionnaire that rates the severity of a depression.

MERIWETHER LEWIS (1774-1809)
AND DEPRESSIVE ILLNESS

Not less than two hours a day should be devoted to exercise and the weather little regarded. I speak this from experience having made this arrangement of my life. If the body is feeble, the mind will not be strong.
—Thomas Jefferson in a letter to Thomas M. Randolph Jr., August 27, 1786

President Thomas Jefferson was a close friend of the Lewis family. He played a vital role in the life of Meriwether Lewis. Meriwether was born in 1774. His father, who was an army officer in the American Revolution, died when Meriwether was only five. (On his way home, lieutenant William Lewis of the Continental army died after his horse fell into an icy stream.)

Meriwether Lewis had joined the Virginia state militia at age twenty. There he was active in putting down the Whiskey Rebellion in Pennsylvania. He continued his military career as an officer in the regular army where he'd meet and befriend his later fellow co-commanding officer, William Clark. Lewis rose to the rank of captain by 1801. Then he accepted an invitation from President Thomas Jefferson, the old family friend, to serve as his private secretary.

Earlier, in 1792, Jefferson had proposed a transcontinental expedition. Lewis had been among the first volunteers, but his youth and inexperience disqualified him. Later, with his frontier experience, Lewis became, in Jefferson's eyes, the perfect candidate. Between 1801 and the appropriation of funds for the expedition in 1803, Lewis studied with members of the faculty at the University of Pennsylvania and gathered information about his proposed route. It would turn out to be a round trip of about four thousand miles. Their means of travel was either by foot or, where necessary, by boat.

We know something of the personality of Lewis through a letter, published in 1814 and written by Thomas Jefferson. The first part of this letter states that Meriwether, from early life . . .

> had been subject to hypochondriac affections. It was a constitutional disposition in all the nearer branches of the family of his name, and was more immediately inherited by him from his father.

What Jefferson was describing was one of the features of a personality tendency vulnerable to major depression, an overconcern and preoccupation with bodily sensations. Besides the hints at a probable hereditary element, Jefferson says furthermore in his letter: "While he lived with me in Washington I observed at times sensible depressions of mind. . . ."

Still, he was the man for the job, having taken intensive courses in medicine, preservation of plant and animal samples, the study of fossils, and the ability to use navigation instruments for determining latitude and longitude.

The expedition began in St. Louis in the spring of 1804, going north through the Mississippi and Missouri Rivers, traversing the Bitterfoot Range (a subrange of the Rocky Mountains running along the border of what is now Montana and Idaho), then by water navigating south down the Columbia River.

All the while the party was challenged physically, rowing against strong river currents and portaging across rugged mountains. All the while, too, they were on guard against Indians. (Jefferson had issued strict orders to be kind and courteous to the Indian tribes they would meet and, most important, need for guidance and sustenance. Some tribes were friendly; some were hostile.)

History would record that the expedition triumphed over nature, the elements, and human limitations by reaching the Pacific Ocean and returning in 1806 over the same route. All but one man survived.

Surely this was an accomplishment that would test body and mind. Their daily activities, furthermore, would exceed the public health exercise recommendations (17.5 kcal/kilogram/week) or the five-mile daily hikes advocated by Dr. Carroll, as they forged the trail from Missouri to Oregon.

We know, from Ambrose's *Undaunted Courage*, some

of Lewis's thoughts, behavior, and actions during the expedition. For example, on the night of his thirty-first birthday, having become the first American citizen to stand at the Continental Divide, he began questioning whether he had, to this time, done enough:

> I have completed my 31st year. I concede that I have, in all probability, now existed about half the period that I have to remain in this world. I reflect that I have as yet done but little, very little indeed, for the heaviness of the human race or to advance the information for the succeeding generation.

At this same time he also wrote:

> The many hours that I have spent in indolence and now sorely feel the want of that information which those hours would have given me, had they been judiciously expended. But the past cannot be recalled. I dash from me the gloomy thought and resolve to redouble my exertions or, in future, to live for mankind, as I am heretofore lived for myself.

Ambrose writes that because he was a man of high energy he was destined to be an explorer, a leader of men, yet despite his high energy (or perhaps as a by-product of it) he was ". . . at times impetuous, but this was tempered by his great self discipline."

The mention of his impetuousness hints at a darker side to Lewis, if not the manic phase of what we call now a bipolar disorder. But his happiest moment would be found when embarking on a great adventure. Said Meriwether Lewis:

> We are now about to penetrate a country at least 2,000 miles in width, on which the foot of civilized man had never trodden . . . I could but esteem this moment of my departure as the most happy of my life.

Ambrose notes, too, that he had a short temper and would act on it, would beat Indians who displeased him, even burn their villages or "expatriate" (banish) them. Jefferson also described "boisterous passions" that he could not keep in check.

Ambrose also remarks about his life after the expedition that ". . . from an active and curious boy he was a hard drinking, hard-riding army officer . . . an overeager governor and speculator in land; a drug taker (opium?) and an alcoholic."

Jefferson wrote, however, that the challenge of the expedition had an overall ameliorating effect on Lewis's otherwise melancholic tendencies:

> During his Western Expedition, the constant exertion which that required of all the faculties of body and mind, suspended these distressing affections; but after his establishment at St. Louis in sedentary occupations, they returned upon him with redoubled vigour [sic], and began seriously to alarm his friends . . .

Even during the journey itself, there were hints of "these distressing affections" when there would be long lapses in Lewis's journal entries.

Soon after the exploration, Jefferson appointed Lewis governor of the Louisiana Territory, a post he assumed in 1808. Within almost two years, his difficulties in this post began to accumulate. He drank heavily. There were personality conflicts. He was a failure in his relationships with women. He quarreled with the territorial secretary and local leaders, and failed to keep his superiors in Washington informed of his policies and plans.

There were questions, too, about his appropriation of government funds. In an attempt to resolve the financial questions, Lewis embarked upon a trip to Washington, D.C., in September 1809. His traveling companions—noting his "melancholy"—feared for his safety.

Staying overnight in Tennessee he apparently shot himself several times with his own weapon. Most historians believe he was a suicide. Jefferson wrote the following:

> At about 3 o'clock in the night [of October 10-11] he did the deed which plunged his friends into affliction and deprived his country of one of her most valued citizens.

In contrasting the vigorous with the sedentary life,

Jefferson was contending that the extreme physical activity Lewis had endured served to ameliorate and neutralize his inherent tendency to depression.

The theme of Jefferson's prescience has matured to where it poses some modern-day questions: Does running (or a similar vigorous aerobic exercise) have a beneficial effect on depressive states and therefore lessen the risk of depression and of suicide? Furthermore, as a corollary, what are the particular mechanisms wherein vigorous, even prodigious, physical exertion affects one's mood?

Can we speculate, too, whether continued extreme physical exercise could have altered the life of Meriwether Lewis? Of course we can speculate. But the validity of it rests with scientific studies and on how we interpret such research. For some understanding, we should first examine a few of the studies of populations, followed by research into the specific mechanism(s) of how exercise affects mood.

In one of the early population studies, individuals were tracked over time to determine the relationship between cardio-respiratory fitness (CRF) and the vulnerability (risk, probability) for depressive symptoms. The Aerobics Center Longitudinal Study in Dallas, Texas, enrolled 11,258 men and 3,085 women.

All participants completed a maximal treadmill exercise test at onset of the study and a follow-up health survey in 1990 and/or 1995. Individuals with a history of a mental disorder, cardiovascular disease, or cancer were excluded. Their CRF was quantified by exercise test duration—how long they could sustain the effort. Depressive symptoms were assessed using a depression questionnaire scale (the twenty-item Center for Epidemiologic Studies Depression Scale, or CES-D).

Those who scored sixteen or more on the CES-D were considered to have depressive symptoms. After an average of twelve years of follow-up, 282 women and 740 men reported depressive symptoms. After making the proper statistical adjustments, the odds (probability) of reporting depressive symptoms was inversely proportional to the degree of CRF. The researchers concluded that a higher CRF is associated with lower risk of depressive symptoms, independent of other clinical risk predictors.

Another early prospective population study followed 8,023 nonhospitalized adults over the age of twenty. The study began in 1965, with data analyzed again in 1974 and 1983. Those who reported a low activity level at the outset were at a greater risk for depression in the first follow-up, compared with those who reported high levels of activity at baseline.

A few years later, in a study of college students exposed to high life stress, those with low physical fitness levels, faced with stressful events, developed more health problems and scored higher on the Beck Depression Inventory compared with those more physically fit.

From the ongoing Harvard/Stanford Alumni study,

Harvard alumni ages thirty-five to seventy-four, were studied in a twenty-three- to twenty-seven-year follow-up. Paffenbarger and colleagues found 387 first attacks of depression among 10,201 alumni; 129 suicides among 21,569 alumni surviving through 1988. Depression rates were lower among those physically active. Suicide, however, was unrelated to antecedent physical activity but substantially higher among men reporting personality traits that predicted increased rates of depression. On the other hand, alumni who regularly participated in sports play had only half the risk of suicide compared with alumni who did not.

All told, this study is supportive of the notion that the sedentary lifeis a risk factor for those predisposed to depression and therefore suicide.

Around the same time, supporting the notion that physical activity has psychological benefits, there was a study smaller but with findings equally significant. Twenty-two medically healthy men, ages forty to sixty, were followed using treadmill data and psychological data in the form of the Minnesota Multiphasic Personality Inventory (MMPI).

The physically active men, eleven in number, had run twenty to sixty minutes, three to six times per week, over three to ten years. The sedentary eleven had not performed physical activity for the last three to ten years.

The eleven physically active men had lower D (depression) ratings than their sedentary counterparts. This was the most important and significant parameter differentiating the active from the sedentary men.

There were other differences. The K scale reflecting high self-concept correlated directly with low body weight. Self-confidence may be a function of physical fitness. Low self-concept is a major component of depressions.

They concluded that when physiologic fitness deteriorates, depression increases; when physiologic fitness is high, depression is low. They also mention that low body weight correlates with high self-concept (K scale).

The researchers also quoted a 1978 article by Dr. Griest's group who, in turn, stated that running has a beneficial effect in terms of other personality characteristics. Among them: mastery of skill and independence, patience and regular effort, capacity for change and self-acceptance, generalized feelings of confidence, distraction from minor problems, altered state of consciousness, pleasure and satisfaction syndrome, and biochemical changes.

The 1978 Griest investigators also mention biochemical reasons. Here they cite the release of endorphins. They speculate that the endorphins mediate satisfaction and reward. Quoting the Stein and Belluzzi hypothesis contending that regular physical activity does maintain elevated levels of endorphins in the central nervous system, they further speculate that endorphins mediate self-confidence.

Enter now the endorphins: What are they and what

is their part in regulation of mood?

Endorphins are protein substances produced in the pituitary gland and in centers of the brain. They are among the opioids—opium-containing substances—produced naturally in the brain.

They were discovered when animal pituitary glands were being ground up in the production of adrenocorticotrophic hormone (ACTH). They come into being via the splitting of the ACTH molecule. Acting in the central nervous system, they are neurohormones. They are the "grease," the lubricants in the transmission of central nervous system impulses and messages. There (the central nervous system, or brain and spinal cord), the endorphins influence the transmission of nerve impulses.

In an elegant study designed to investigate the biochemical mechanism of the "runner's high" hypothesis —"runner's high" being anything from excitement to euphoria to altered sense perceptions induced by long runs—researchers in Germany conducted the following experiment.

Ten trained male athletes were recruited. Their age range was thirty-three to forty. Their experience running ensured that they were easily able to run steadily for at least two hours, having run at least four hours a week for the past two years.

After at least twenty-four hours of inactivity, the athletes were injected with a radioactive substance that had opioid properties but only mild stimulating potential. Because of its molecular composition, it was destined to go to the same receptor sites as would the naturally produced opioids. At the same time of injection, a PET scan (positron emission tomography; it is used to determine tissue and organ functioning) was taken in order to map the destinations of the radioactive substance. At the same time the PET scan and injection were done, the subjects took a psychological test of mood in the form of a Visual Analog Mood Scale (VAMS).

At least one week later the subjects were asked to run for two hours. Then thirty minutes after the cessation of the run, there was another PET scan taken along with simultaneous injection of the radioactive chemical. And again the subjects took the VAMS.

What they found upon the second injection/PET scan administration was that the initial sites of receptor acceptance were essentially blocked. The sites where the radioactive injected substance (termed a "ligand") initially migrated to in the twenty-four-hour post-activity experiment done a week earlier now would not accept the radioactive molecules. Inferred from this was that the receptor sites had become flooded by their rightful users, the natural opioids—the endorphins—whose occupation of the receptor sites was stimulated by the run.

Furthermore, on the VAMSs, the parameters of euphoria and happiness were the ones that were enhanced following the two-hour run. And finally, the areas the endorphins had apparently flooded were located in prefrontal (short-term memory, selective attention, judgment) and limbic (functions of emotion, behavior, long-term memory) brain regions.

Thus we have proof, albeit circumstantial, for the opioid explanation for the phenomenon known as runner's high.

Such should not mean that this is the sole biochemical component of the high. Also involved are the very neurohormones that the antidepressant drugs activate, including serotonin. In one study, brains of exercising rats were found to have increases in the breakdown products of serotonin.

So far, what proofs now do we have for the benefits of exercise vis-à-vis depressive states, and what are the mechanisms involved?

From the studies of groups of people we can be certain that fitness correlates inversely with incidence of depression and suicide. Fitness correlates directly with self-esteem, and positive self-esteem correlates inversely with depressive states. The most important test variable using the MMPI, separating fit from unfit individuals, is the D (depression) scale. Fit people are less depressed than unfit and the biological mechanism where running evokes a "high" involves an increased production and flooding of receptor sites for the naturally occurring opioid neurohormones (endorphins) and of other naturally produced neurohormones, e.g., serotonin. These flood the brain regions that regulate emotional states.

We can also confirm with conviction, that Jefferson's contention that if the body is feeble, the mind will not be strong, was scientifically accurate.

However, speculations that endorphins mediate satisfaction and self-confidence apply to Meriwether while he was vigorously exercising, but not his sedentary life. Lewis was the proverbial fish out of water while among the sedentary, lacking an avenue to direct his otherwise potentially powerful and productive "faculties of body and mind."

His faculties were stimulated both by the exertion needed for the enterprise at hand, and perhaps even more so by the mental perception of the magnitude and glory of the task at hand, that is, to explore new territory. Perhaps the pot of gold, the "reward" at the end of this rainbow, would be the discovery of the Northwest Passage to the Pacific.

This perception would prove to be both energizing and depressing, for with all he accomplished, at the very end he was disappointed, probably depressed, at not finding the fabled passageway. The 1978 Griest investigators' contention that the endorphins mediate satisfaction and reward must have failed for Lewis, for he had not found that fabled passageway and the satisfaction that would have accompanied that discovery.

Even during the journey itself, there were hints of "these distressing affections" when there came long lapses in Lewis's journal entries. At the same time, he was a man of discipline and fortitude, a man with a lofty goal acting to stimulate and counteract the draining tugs from his underlying depressive tendencies, and, on balance, he was able to function and act at a high level.

His "most happy" moment was at the beginning of his trip—the very moment he began this venture. So we have a hint that it is not only exercise that produces a type of runner's high engendered by the endorphins, but also our thoughts, expectations, and hopes. And, conversely, there *are* opioid receptor centers in the brain, activated by endorphins but also activated by sad thoughts, that mediate depressed mood states—the very states that Meriwether must have felt at journey's end when his expectations were dashed as he perceived an absence of reward.

It would seem, therefore, that sad thoughts or unhappy memories can activate sad and depressive feelings. It seems, too, that there is a biochemical mechanism for such a phenomenon. Yet this seems to pose a puzzling dichotomy where endogenous opioids encourage both euphoria and depression. But it is not so puzzling when we realize that morphine, depending on dose and site of reception, does the same, bringing about either a "high" or a depression of functions. Furthermore, this opposing action would also seem to vindicate the premise of Cognitive Behavioral Therapy (CBT): that thoughts influence emotions and emotions can influence thoughts, that there is a continuum among thoughts, ideas, and feelings, with a corresponding biochemical mechanism to these interactions.

Gina Kolata, science journalist for the *New York Times*, interviewed the lead researcher in the runner's high opioid hypothesis study. Writing about the interview in the *Times*, she quoted Dr. Henning Boecker, who noted that the brain areas that were stimulated (limbic and prefrontal areas) ". . . are activated when people are involved in romantic love affairs or," he added, "when you hear music that gives you a chill of euphoria, like Rachmaninoff's Piano Concerto No. 3."

Not only can music bring about a state of euphoria, but some of the composers of classical music also have found inspiration and emotional balance from vigorous exercise. There is likely a reciprocal reverberating relationship between exercise and creativity. (Note, too, how musical conductors undergo vigorous and sustained upper-body workouts while leading their orchestras.)

If the endorphin response can be elicited from music, perhaps through exercise it has also inspired and provided the same emotional balance to composers of classic music. One such classical composer was Gustav Mahler.

NOTES

His father . . . died when Meriwether was only five. . . Freudian psychoanalysts believe that there is a higher rate of depression and suicide in male children whose fathers die when the child is at ages five to seven, the Oedipal stage. They theorize that at this age, awakening in the male child are feelings of rivalry with his father for the mother's love and attention, with accompanying unconscious death wishes toward the father. Thus, if the father does die or leave, then the seeds of guilt are planted, as if wishing made it so.

had been subject to hypochondriac affections . . . Meriwether Lewis and William Clark. *History of the Expedition Under the Command of Captains Lewis and Clark.* Edited by Nicholas Boiddle and Paul Allen. Philadelphia: Bradford and Inskeep, 1814. Here Jefferson was referring to hypochondriasis, a chronic preoccupation with bodily sensations with excessive worry of having a serious disease. This state is not uncommon in people who develop depressive illnesses.

While he lived with me in Washington . . . Ibid.

I have completed my 31st year. . . . S. E. Ambrose, *Undaunted Courage: Meriwether Lewis, Thomas Jefferson and the Opening of the American West.* New York: Simon & Schuster, 1996.

The many hours that I have spent in indolence . . . Ibid.
at times impetuous . . . Ibid.

We are now about to penetrate a country . . . Ibid

During his Western Expedition . . . Lewis and Clark, *History of the Expedition.*

Even during the journey itself . . . Ambrose, *Undaunted Courage.*

Most historians believe he was a suicide. There has been debate over the years whether Lewis was a suicide or a murder victim. In 2003, a University of Iowa counseling psychology professor, John S. Westefeld, and graduate student Aaron Less wrote an essay, "Meriwether Lewis: Was It Suicide?" They concluded that Lewis very likely committed suicide. Their article was accepted for publication in *Suicide and Life-Threatening Behavior*, the official journal of the American Association of Suicidology.

In their essay, they used a risk factor model for suicide assessment developed by Heriberto Sanchez. Westefeld and Less found that the preponderance of evidence—including Lewis's previous attempts to take his own life—indicates that he was susceptible to suicide.

At about 3 o'clock in the night . . . Lewis and Clark, *History of the Expedition*.

In one of the early population studies . . . . Xuemei Sui, James N. Laditka, Timothy S. Church, James W. Hardin, Nancy Chase, Keith Davis, Steven N. Blair. Prospective study of cardio-respiratory fitness and depressive symptoms in women and men. *J Psych Res*, October 2008.

Another early prospective population study . . . T. C. Camacho, R. E. Roberts, N. B. Lazarus, G. A. Kaplan, R. D. Cohen. Physical activity and depression: Evidence from the Alameda County Study. *Am J Epidemiol* 1991; 134:220-31.

a study of college students exposed to high life stress . . . D. L. Roth, D. S. Holmes. Influence of physical fitness in determining the impact of stressful life events on physical and psychologic health. *Psychosom Med* 1985; 47(2):164-173.

Beck Depression Inventory: This is a twenty-one-question multiple-choice self-report inventory often used to determine the severity of depression.

From the ongoing Harvard/Stanford Alumni study . . . Ralph S. Paffenbarger Jr., I. M. Lee. A natural history of athleticism, health and longevity. 1998; *J Sports Sci*, 16:S31-S45.

supporting the notion that physical activity has psychological benefits . . . D. Lobstein et al., Depression as a powerful discriminator between physically active and sedentary middle-aged men. *J Psychosom Med* 1983; 27:69-76.

Minnesota Multiphasic Personality Inventory (MMPI) consists of over five hundred true/false questions where responses, usually computer scored, measure a number of symptoms among them depression, paranoia, hypochondriasis, and schizophrenia.

The researchers also quoted a 1978 article by Dr. Griest's group . . . J. H. Griest, M. H. Klein, R. R. Eischens, I. Faris, A. S. Gurman, W. P. Morgan. Running through your mind. J Psychosom Res 1978; 22:259.

Quoting the Stein and Belluzzi hypothesis . . . L. Stein, J. D. Belluzzi. Brain endorphins and the sense of well-being: a psychobiological hypothesis. In *The Endorphins: Advances in Biochemistry and Psychopharmacology* (Edited by E. Costa and M. Trabucci). 1978; 18:299.

Endorphins influence by attaching themselves to receptors lying on the membrane of nerve fibers. Essentially there are specific receptor sites on nerve fiber membranes for specific molecules, analogous to reserved parking places. Morphine, for example, has specific receptor sites in specific areas of the brain where it can "park" and fit onto nerve membranes in a lock-and-key fashion. It is similarly so for the naturally producing endorphins. (The *en* is derived from *endogenous*, and the *orphin* from *morphine-like*.) To fulfill the definition of an endorphin, the substance must provide pain relief, and that same pain relief must be neutralized by an opioid receptor antagonist (naloxone). In other words, an antagonist here (naloxone) is the substance that blocks the entry of the endorphin molecule into its natural reserved place on the membrane of the nerve cell, the very site where the endorphin molecules influence the nerve impulse.

"runner's high" being anything from excitement to euphoria . . . A more detailed definition: *Runner's high* has been defined as a "euphoric sensation experienced through running, usually unexpected, in which the runner feels a heightened sense of well being, enhanced appreciation of nature, and transcendence of barriers of time and place." M. L. Sachs. The runner's high. In *Running as Therapy: An Integrated Approach, edited by M. L. Sachs and G. W. Buffone. Lincoln: University of*

Nebraska Press, 1984.

researchers in Germany conducted the following experiment: H. Boecker, T. Sprenger, M. E. Spilker, G. Henriksen, M. Koppenhoefer, K. J. Wagner, M. Valet, A. Berthele, T. R. Tolle. The runner's high: opiodergic mechanisms in the human brain. *Cereb Cortex.* Nov; 18(11):2523-31.

a PET scan (positron emission tomography) . . . A PET scan is used to characterize the metabolism of normal and diseased organs or tissues in order to determine how they are functioning.

This technique involves the use of nuclear medicine imaging in which a radioactive tracer, such as fluoridated glucose, is injected or inhaled. The radiotracer element gives off energy in the form of small positively charged particles called positrons. The positrons released by the tracer are positively charged electrons, the anti-particles to electrons. When positrons and electrons collide they are annihilated, releasing two gamma ray photons moving in opposite directions at the speed of light. The PET scanner detects this radiation.

The gamma ray photons are then detected by the PET camera taking pictures of the tissue areas where the tracer accumulates, and a computer generates three-dimensional body images. Bodily organs or tissues with the highest metabolic rates absorb the most glucose and are easily visualized in the PET scan images. Measured are certain body functions such as blood flow, and glucose (sugar) metabolism, the purpose of which is to determine how certain organs and tissues are functioning.

Visual Analog Mood Scale (VAMS). . . The VAMS measures eight specific mood states: Afraid, Confused, Sad, Angry, Energetic, Tired, Happy, and Tense.

Test materials include the Professional Manual, the VAMS Response Booklet, and a metric ruler. A pen or pencil is also required for administration. Respondents indicate the point along the vertical line that best describes how they are currently feeling.

The VAMS can be used for a variety of applications including repeated assessment of mood states to monitor treatment efficacy, screening for mood disorder in primary care settings, and screening for mood disorder in patients with neurologic illness.

In one study, brains of exercising rats . . . F. Chaouloff Physical exercise and brain monoamines: a review. *Acta Physiol Scand* 1989; 137:1-13.

The 1978 Griest investigators' contention . . . Griest, et. al. Running through your mind.

And, conversely, there *are* opioid receptor centers . . . R. J. Bodnar. Endogenous opiates and behavior: 2006. *Peptides*, 2007; 28:2435-2513

Writing about the interview in the *Times* . . . Exercise test: truth or myth? March 27, 2008.

INTELLECT AND CREATIVITY:

**The Role of Exercise in the Lives of
a Classical Music Composer,
Two Poet-Philosophers
and a Renaissance Man**

Gustav Mahler (1860-1911), Bohemian-born but living most of his life in Austria, was both composer and conductor. During his lifetime he was considered one of the leading orchestral and operatic conductors of the day. At the same time, as part of an enduring pattern of rejection and loss, he was never fully accepted by the musical establishment. One reason was the strong anti-Semitic sentiment of his day and of his immediate milieu—despite his conversion to Roman Catholicism. Another reason was his difficult personality; he often alienated his musicians along with the musical hierarchy of the day.

Working his way up as conductor in the opera house pecking order, he became conductor of the Hamburg Opera from 1891 to 1897. A major tragedy during that time was the suicide of his equally talented composer brother, Otto, at age twenty-five. In 1897, Mahler, then thirty-seven, was offered the directorship

Gustav Mahler.

of the Vienna Opera, the most prestigious musical position in the Austrian empire.

In 1902 Mahler married Alma Schindler, twenty
years younger than he (she would outlive him by more
than half a century). Alma was also a musician and
composer, but typical of his personality, Mahler forbade her to engage in any creative work.

A daughter, Maria Anna, was born in 1902, and another daughter, Anna Justine, was born in 1904.
Tragedy struck the family when in 1906 at age four,

Maria died from diphtheria. In the weeks following her death, Mahler was diagnosed with heart disease and the doctor forbade any further exercise. Up to that time, Mahler was an ardent exerciser. In her book published in 1946, Alma Mahler described the doctor's forbidding him to exercise and the effect its absence had on Mahler's life:

> He forbade him to walk uphill, or bicycle, or swim; indeed he was so blind as to order a course of training to teach him to walk at all; first it was to be five minutes, then ten, and so on until he was used to walking; and this for a man who was accustomed to *violent exercise* [author's italics]!
>
> And Mahler did as he was told. Watch in hand, he accustomed himself to walking—and forgot the life he had lived up to that fatal hour.

For Mahler, said Professor Robert Greenberg of the San Francisco Conservatory of Music, "this was a death sentence, a physical and emotional death sentence."

Up to that time he had engaged in long hours of walking or rowing. Alma wrote about his "hot walks" regimen:

> We walked for three or four hours, or else we rowed over the dazzling water, which reflected the glare of the sun. Sometimes I was too exhausted to go on . . . Often and often he stood still . . . and taking out a small notebook ruled for music, wrote and reflected, and wrote again, sometimes beating time in the air. . . . *Then we*

went on or turned for home if, as often happened,
he was eager to get back to his studio with all speed
[author's italics].

In 1910, still grief-stricken over his daughter's tortured death from diphtheria, Mahler lost his position as conductor of the Metropolitan Opera to Toscanini. Beset with rumors of his wife's infidelity, he consulted with fellow Austrian Sigmund Freud. Accompanying Mahler, ironically on a four-hour walk in the woods, the father of psychoanalysis diagnosed Mahler with an "obsessional neurosis." For Gustav Mahler, a man forever ruminating over universal questions of life and death, pursuing extreme exercise was consistent with a study showing that those who felt the cognitive concomitants of anxiety, worry and ruminations, sought out vigorous exercise, whereas those who had the more physiologic signs such as palpitations and sweating engaged in relaxation programs.

Soon after the meeting with Freud, he returned to America to conduct the New York Philharmonic Orchestra. In February 1911, while conducting during a demanding concert season, he was overcome with a systemic streptococcal infection and seen by a leading cardiologist of the day, Dr. Emanuel Libman of New York's Mount Sinai Hospital, Libman made a diagnosis of "infective endocarditis." (Later this was called "sub-acute bacterial endocarditis.")

Mahler returned to Europe; he was unresponsive to a new serum. His heart condition and general physical state continued to deteriorate. He would later return to Vienna, and in May 1911 he died.

Attending Mahler's funeral, symphony conductor Bruno Walter described the weather as they laid the coffin in the cemetery. Walter wrote that a storm broke with such a torrential downpour that the proceedings were almost halted. An immense silent crowd followed the hearse. At the very moment the coffin was lowered, the sun then broke through the clouds.

The weather at the funeral was metaphor for Mahler's spiritual and nature-loving side, but also for his profound bouts of melancholy. His exercise regimens were, in part, his questing for musical inspiration. The notes he may have heard in his head, generated by the endorphin surges and the rhythm of his pace, became augmented by the "chill of euphoria" as Dr. Henning Boecker described. It was probably music composed in Mahler's mind that made him hurry back to his studio so that he could integrate the newly heard notes into the score of his musical manuscript.

Just as exercise stimulated Mahler's musical composing, artful prose, too, can be generated during the course of vigorous exercise, like brisk walking or rowing. So attention turns now to another artist, one who was both poet and philosopher, who spent much time in nature's bosom and whose prose evokes excitement in all of us.

We are all stirred reading or hearing Henry David

Thoreau's conclusion written in *Walden*: "If a man does not keep pace with his companions perhaps it is because he hears a different drummer. Let him step to the music he hears, however measured or far away." The Bard of Walden took many steps, literally so, during his sojourn into nature—the wilderness surrounding Walden Pond. And while he took those steps, he carried his notebook so that he could frame his thoughts into beautiful phrases.

In the spring of 1845, Thoreau had built a hut for himself on the shores of Walden Pond—a small lake then about a mile and a half south of Concord village. Except for occasional visits from friends and walks into the village, until September 1847 he lived there alone.

As best as can be determined, Thoreau would walk half a mile from his cabin to the road, then another mile into Concord village, making a round trip of three miles. Like Mahler who during his "hot walks" was seen to be taking out ":a small notebook ruled for music," most afternoons Thoreau would walk, pen and notebook in hand, from 2:30 to 5:30 P.M. "to see what I've caught in my traps which I set for facts."

Assuming this regimen for six days a week, the poet-philosopher would earn thirty-six aerobic points a week, six above what Dr. Kenneth Cooper considered necessary for fitness.

Thomas Jefferson, along with Dr. Carroll, would certainly pronounce him fit. Thoreau, fulfilling public health parameters for fitness, had a bit to say about

Sketch of Thoreau on his walk with notebook.

fitness and mind when he penned the following passages:

> I never feel that I am inspired unless my body is also. They are fatally mistaken who think while they strive with their minds that they may suffer their bodies to stagnate in luxury and sloth.
>
> The body is the first proselyte the soul makes. The whole duty of man may be expressed in one line . . . make to yourself a healthy body.
>
> I think that I cannot preserve my health and spirits, unless I spend four hours a day at least— and it is commonly more than that—sauntering through the woods and over the hills and fields, absolutely free from all worldly engagements.

Thoreau jotted down his observations of the countryside, and here we may have the first description of the runner's high. Thoreau wrote, "The fashions of the wood are more fluctuating than those of Paris. Snow, rime, ice, green and dry leaves incessantly make new patterns. There are all shapes and hues of the kaleidoscope . . . Every time I see a nodding pine top, it seems as if a new fashion of wearing plumes has come into vogue."

Compare this with a description of the runner's high, a "euphoric sensation experienced during running, usually unexpected, in which the runner feels a heightened sense of well-being, enhanced appreciation of nature, and transcendence of barriers of time and place."

How much walking or running is needed to bring about this alteration of senses? The phenomenon of runner's high is more easily and perhaps more accurately measured in terms of duration of effort rather than in distance. Psychiatrist Dr. Thaddeus Kostrubala observed that when one runs about thirty minutes, "the senses seem to increase in alertness." And the first one of the senses that seems to be stimulated, according to Kostrubala, is the visual.

As for the senses, Joseph Wood Krutch referred to the "unity of sensibility"—something characteristic of the English writers of the seventeenth century, something previously lost but recaptured in Thoreau's writings—implying ". . . the ability to perceive and to present the totality of an experience in such a way that the distinction between the playful and the grave, the comic and the serious, the poetic and the prosaic, the religious and the secular, disappears and the whole complex total is present at once."

Krutch could actually be describing the blending of right-brain ("poetic") and left-brain ("prosaic") functions, something Kostrubala has referred to, and something researcher Hatfield and colleagues examined. They found that fit older men, compared with unfit older and younger men (all groups were given a battery of mental tests), scored more efficiently in both left- and right- brain cognitive functions than did the older and younger untrained, unfit men.

Additionally, researcher Dustman in Salt Lake City was exercise testing for neuromuscular coordination in a group of exercising subjects; as a by-product he also found that as their fitness expanded, so did their IQs. The investigators found improvement in other cognitive tests as well, all of this following a four-month exercise program. There were both aerobic fitness groups and strength and flexibility training groups, the former group, showing a higher degree of improvement although the latter group's improvement was statistically significant. The control non-exercise group demonstrated no improvement.

There are a few more explanations of this emotional calm and intellectual balm that we call runner's high.

To determine whether attention deficits associated

with the aging process could be reversed with significant improvements in cardiovascular function, researcher Hawkins and his group concluded that long-term fitness did indeed have a significant positive effect on cognitive abilities, but that short-term fitness programs produced only equivocal results.

They also set out to prove that short-term exercise programs, producing significant changes in cardiovascular function, could have equally positive effects on those functions in the aging that had the most room for improvement. Those functions were the ones where divided attention was required, that is, the so-called ability to chew gum and walk at the same time. What they did show was that following a ten-week exercise program, the older exercisers showed substantially more improvements in tasks requiring divided attention and also on single task performances than did non-exercising controls.

The areas of the brain thought to be the seat of the functions of attention flexibility are the frontal lobes. And with an enhancement of cardiovascular function, as a result of aerobic exercise, bringing more blood to the frontal lobes, a link between exercise and cognitive function in the aging can tentatively be made.

With this increased blood supply engendered by exercise may also come elevated levels of brain-derived neurotrophic factor (BDNF), a substance that supports the function and survival of many neurons (nerve cells—functional units of the nervous system—conducting impulses), possibly protecting them from free radical damage. (Free radicals are breakdown products of cells that carry an electrical charge, in turn damaging other cells.) Exercising rats were found to have enhanced levels of BDNF in areas of their brains following exercise as compared with sedentary controls.

It is not frivolous to consider that the connections among exercise, blood supply to the brain, and improved cognitive functioning are salient when you consider that while the brain is only 2 percent of our total weight, it still receives 15 percent of its total blood flow, while using 15 percent of its oxygen and 70 percent of available glucose.

And what did Thoreau in his walks in the fresh air of Walden Pond have to say about breathing the fresh air? "Of all ebriosity," he wrote in *Walden*, "who does not prefer to be intoxicated by the air he breathes." This might illustrate another prescient connection between physical fitness and mental acuity. Note also that poet John Dryden once wrote, "Toil strung the nerves and purified the blood."

Walking was a passion for another poet, William Wordsworth (1790-1850). Like Thoreau he would also have a "trap for facts" when he walked every morning and brought back home "a large treat." According to his sister, the "large treat" meant lines of poetry. By the time he was sixty-five, it was estimated that Wordsworth had walked 180,000 miles. In walks of two to three hours, from nowhere in particular wrote another poet, Alfred Housman, ("To an Athlete Dying Young") following a long walk, ". . . there would flow into my mind, with sudden and unaccountable emotion, sometimes a line or two of verse, sometimes a stanza at once." Possibly this flow of emotion and outpouring of verse had something to do with the rhythms aroused by walking.

The philosopher Friedrich Nietzsche summed up the poets' penchant for walking: "All truly great thoughts," he has been quoted, "are conceived while walking."

Combining literature and science, politics and statesmanship, we have guerrilla fighter, lawyer, botanist, military general, scientist, prime minister of South Africa, framer of the League of Nations and the United Nations and onetime president of the General Assembly of the United Nations Jan Christiaan Smuts (1870-1950).

Graduating from college with honors in both literature and science, Smuts viewed personality as an integrated whole. Publication of his classic work lagged a good forty years. Finally his treatise *Holism and Evolution* ushered in the concept of holistic medicine.

Daily vigorous exercise was an integral part of his lifestyle. His long walks were at a pace of three and a half miles an hour, with three-hour climbs up to the top of Table Mountain and then descents eschewing the cable car. His son described his long swims: "Phys-

Jan Smuts

ical exercise," he wrote, "formed quite a fetish in my father's life."

Mahler, Thoreau, Wordsworth, and Housman knew great creativity during their exercising journeys; Smuts' experience was similar. His son noted:

> From his walks he would come back sun-tanned and wet with perspiration, not fatigued (for he had amazing stamina) *but just nicely tired and contented, and at peace with the world* [author's italics]. With the quickening of his pulses

during the walking he had been able to get a clearer perspective of things and had solved the problems he had had in mind at the start.

A devastating "problem" in and of the mind, specifically traumatic brain injury, will be explored in the next chapter.

NOTES

In her book published in 1946, Alma Mahler . . . A. Mahler. *Gustav Mahler, Memories and Letters*. New York: Viking Press, 1946.

He forbade him to walk uphill, or bicycle . . . Ibid.

For Mahler, said Professor Robert Greenberg . . . *Greenberg Lectures*, Lecture No. 45.

Alma wrote about his "hot walks" regimen: Mahler, *Gustav Mahler*.

For Gustav Mahler . . . pursuing extreme exercise . . . R. C. Casper. Exercise and mood *W Rev Nutr Dietet*. 1993; 71:115-43.

. . . the father of psychoanalysis diagnosed Mahler . . . Ernest Jones. *Sigmund Freud: Life and Work*. London: Hogarth Press, 1953-1957.

" . . . pursuing extreme exercise was consistent with a study showing . . . Casper, Exercise and mood.

"to see what I've caught in my traps which I set for facts" . . . In 1873, Ellery Channing (1818-1901), Thoreau's friend of twenty years, wrote a biography, *Thoreau, the Poet-Naturalist*: "During many years he used the afternoon for walking, and usually set forth about half past two, returning at half past five," said Channing, who also wrote about Thoreau's carrying a notebook and a small magnifying glass, in order, Thoreau said, "'to see what I've caught in my traps which I set for facts.'"

six above what Dr. Kenneth Cooper considered necessary for fitness. Kenneth H. Cooper, M.D., M.P.H., *The New Aerobics.* New York: M. Evans, 1970, pp. 172-7.

I never feel that I am inspired unless my body is also . . . *Journal,* June 21, 1840.

The body is the first proselyte the soul makes. Ibid.

I think that I cannot preserve my health . . . *Journal,* April 26, 1841.

The fashions of the wood . . . . J. W. Krutch, editor. *Thoreau: Walden and Other Writings.* A Bantam Classic, 13th edition, 1979.

Compare this with a description of the runners high . . . Sachs ML: The Runner's High in Sachs ML, Buffone GW (eds); *Running as Therapy: An Integrated Approach.* Lincoln, University of Nebraska Press. 1984.

Psychiatrist Dr. Thaddeus Kostrubala observed . . . . Kostrubala T: *The Joy of Running.* New York, JB Lippincott 1976.

And the first one of the senses . . . Ibid.

the ability to perceive and to present . . . Krutch, editor *Thoreau.*

They found that fit older men . . . B. Hatfield; B. A. Slater, D. L. SantaMaria; & A. J. Krotz. Aerobic training is associated with increased central nervous system efficiency in older trained males. Abstract of a paper presented at the meeting of the North American Society for the Psychology of Sport and Physical Activity, Pittsburgh, 1992.

Dustman in Salt Lake City was exercise testing . . . R. E. Dustman; R. O. Ruhling; E. M. Russell; D. E. Shearer; H. W. Bonekat; J. W. Shigeoka; J. S. Wood; & D. C. Bradford. Aerobic exercise training and improved neuropsychological functions in older individuals. *Neurobiol Ag* 1984; 5: 35-42.

. . . **long-term fitness did indeed have a significant positive effect** . . . H. L. Hawkins; D. Capaldi; A. F. Kramer; Aging, Exercise and Attention *Psych ag* 1992; 7: 643-653.

elevated levels of brain-derived neurotrophic factor (BDNF) . . . T. P. LaFontaine, T. M. DiLorenzo, P. A.Frensch, R. C. Stucky-Ropp, E. P. Bargman, D. G. McDonald. Aerobic exercise and mood: a brief review, 1985-1990. *Sports Med* 1992; 13: 160-170.

Exercising rats were found to have enhanced levels of BDNF . . . . E. A. Neeper, J. Choi Gomez-Pinilla, C. Cotman. Exercise and brain neurotrophins *Nature* Jan. 12, 1995.

It is not frivolous to consider that the connections . . . H. B. Simon. *Staying Well. Your Complete Guide to Disease Prevention.* Boston: Houghton Mifflin, 1992.

Ebriosity is an old term, not even in modern dictionaries. It simply meant a state of drunkenness.

According to his sister the "large treat" . . . *Gettysburg Rev*, winter 1998; 2(4).

Possibly this flow of emotion . . . Ibid.

"All truly great thoughts are conceived while walking." This is not exactly what Nietzsche actually wrote. In his 1895 publication, *Twilight of the Idols*, in the chapter Maxims and Arrows Number 34, the last two lines read: "The sedentary life is the very sin against the Holy Spirit. Only thoughts reached by walking have value."

Finally his treatise *Holism and Evolution* . . . J. C. Smuts, *Holism and Evolution.* New York: Macmillan, 1926.

"Physical exercise," he wrote . . . J. C. Smuts, *Jan Christiaan Smuts: A Biography.* William Morrow & Co., 1952.

. . . **and had solved the problems he had had in mind at the start** . . . Ibid. This phenomenon of clarification of thought has been described by many exercise-enthusiast writers, usually runners. It comes about, in all likelihood, from a combination of processes motored by vigorous exercise. Some call it the clearing out of "mental garbage."

Specifically, this sharpening of thought may be related to regulation of blood glucose through exercise along with the consequent increased blood flow to essential areas in the brain associated with cognitive processes, particularly the hippocampus and its subregion, the dentate nucleus. A. C. Pereira, D. E. Huddleston, A. M. Brickman, et al. An in vivo correlate of exercise-induced neurogenesis in the adult dentate gyrus. *Proc Natl Acad Sci USA* 2007;104:5638-5643

EXERCISE AND TRAUMATIC BRAIN INJURY

The Central Park Jogger—
A Story of Hope and Possibility

Shortly after 9 P.M. on April 19, 1989, in Manhattan's Central Park, twenty-eight-year-old Trisha Meili, associate in the Corporate Finance Department of Salomon Brothers Inc., a Phi Beta Kappa graduate of Wellesely College holding a Yale graduate business/international relations degree, was about to gain an alias, the Central Park Jogger. She was rendered unconscious and comatose after being raped, bludgeoned, bound, gagged, and left to die.

Parts of her story, as summarized below, come from personal correspondence and informal conversation. Most, however, is gleaned from portions of her bestselling book, *I Am the Central Park Jogger: A Story of Hope and Possibility* (New York: Scribner, 2003). The book contains her search for facts about this period, culled from newspaper, hospital, and doctor reports, and from interviews with medical personnel who had treated her. From these accounts she began to learn what had happened, given that she had no recall for the event and for the weeks that followed.

Trisha described what happened to her as an "extraordinary trauma." It was rather a totally horrendous devastating trauma. This summary will be focusing particularly on the role of exercise in her rehabilitation from extensive brain damage.

Before this night, Trisha had run three Boston Marathons (best time 3:40) and many 10k races. She was *determined* to run that night (April 19), determination and compulsivity being characteristic features of her makeup. Her last memory, before the run—she entered the park at 84th Street and would run uptown to the poorly lit 102nd Street crossover—was a five-o'clock phone call. Then there is a void in recall until six weeks later.

As she ran along the 102nd Street drive that crossed through the park, she was dragged down into a ravine. Trisha Meili was punched, kicked, raped, hit in the left side of her face with a brick or rock; her eye socket was shattered. Three and a half hours later, unresponsive, bleeding profusely, eye puffed out and almost closed, she was found in a ravine in Central Park lying prone with "airway compromise respirations."

During the ambulance ride to Metropolitan Hospital the EMTs were unable to get an accurate blood pressure reading. She was hypothermic with a body temperature of eighty-five degrees. There were five deep cuts on her face. Her skull was fractured; her arms and legs were flailing violently, indicative of "massive brain damage."

Upon admission to Metropolitan she was graded on

the Glasgow Coma Scale (3-15), a commonly used neurological scale. Fifteen is normal consciousness and brain function; three is totally unresponsive or just being alive. Trisha was graded 4-5 because she did have eye responses.

There was extreme swelling of her brain. "Permanent brain damage seems inevitable," read a portion of the admitting note to Metropolitan Hospital. Her face was unrecognizable to a friend who came to identify her. The attempt to remove a breathing tube eight days later was unsuccessful. She was comatose for twelve days. On the fourteenth day a memo was sent to employees at Salomon to the effect that she has been removed from the ventilator and could utter single- and two-word phrases.

On May 1 Trisha had begun to awaken from her coma. She began to identify simple words on flash cards, could say "hello" to her father, and could move her eyebrows voluntarily. "She still suffers moments of delusion and fluctuates between lucid and unresponsive," read her chart. Also she had pneumonia with a temperature of 106 and was "not well oriented to time and place." But on May 9 she was noted to be better oriented to time and place.

Two weeks post-coma, her chart read: ". . . signs of severe cognitive dysfunction suggestive of widespread cerebral impairment . . . At this point she manifests limitations in all areas of cognitive functioning . . . The severity of the patient's condition causes serious concerns about her prospects for long-term recovery. However, it is far too early to make predictions concerning outcome."

Dr. Kurtz, director of Surgical Intensive Care Unit, had thought she had less than a 50 percent chance of recovering normal brain function. He had told the family that chances for life were 50 percent and that severe brain damage was likely.

Her first clear memory was May 26 when she told a loquacious visitor friend to "shut up."

On June 7, seven weeks after the attack, she arrived at Gaylord Rehabilitation Hospital, a 109-bed non-profit long-term, acute care hospital for adults in the hills of Wallingford, Connecticut. She was then unable to work the buttons on her shirt, unable to walk, unable to remember where to go for therapy sessions. She felt devastated by her failure to remember what she'd read a second ago or think on any but the most rudimentary level.

Her treatment was multifocused using varied modalities, not the least of these would be the compassionate approach of the total staff. Exercise was at first focused on relearning balance and how to walk. Then one fine day in August she encountered a chapter of the Achilles Track Club at Gaylord.

Achilles is a worldwide organization that both organizes and encourages people with all kinds of disabilities—amputation, arthritis, cancer, cerebral palsy, cystic fibrosis, multiple sclerosis, paraplegia, stroke, traumatic brain injury, and visual impairment—to participate in running. Its beginning was in the 1970s, the inspiration of Dr. Richard Traum, himself an amputee.

For her first run at Gaylord with the Achilles group, she tried to run a hilly quarter-mile loop. She described her initial difficulties with this course, and her final navigation of it, an accomplishment that to her seemed monumental. She wrote:

> And, oh, it felt good! I was acutely aware I was taking back something that belonged to me but had been taken away: the joy of running.

Three months later and seven months after the incident, she walked out of Gaylord, ready to face the world, including a return to full duty at Salomon Brothers.

And what of Trisha Meili today? Here, as the late Paul Harvey might put it, is the rest of the story.

In September 1996, she married. She left Salomon Brothers in 1998. In a total career change, she became president of The Bridge Fund of New York, Inc., a nonprofit organization whose mission was to prevent homelessness of the working poor who are threatened with the loss of their housing but do not qualify for government assistance.

Trisha continued to work with the Achilles International. After her encounter with the Gaylord Hospital chapter, she had returned to New York and continued to get stronger. She met founder Dr. Dick

Traum and became an Achilles guide at Saturday workouts in the early 1990s. She then became a board member in 1995 and was elected the first chair of Achilles in 2001. In addition, she also became a board member of Gaylord and is now secretary of the board. Finally, she became an advocate trainer of SAVI, Mount Sinai Hospital's Sexual Assault and Violence Intervention Program.

In the spring of 2001 Trisha left The Bridge Fund. Soon after that, she spoke at Spaulding Rehabilitation Hospital about her injury and recovery to a group of physicians, clinicians, brain-injured patients, and families. It was for Trisha Meili a profound moment. It convinced her that she needed to share her story of recovery and healing in a more public way. In the fall of 2001 she began to write her book. Once it was written and published, as a result of speaking requests from all kinds of organizations, she became a motivational speaker.

Despite at times having trouble finding the right word, having lost her sense of smell, with occasional difficulty with balance and inability to multitask as well as she was once able, nevertheless she says in her book, "As it turned out, the attack, meant to take my life, gave me a deeper life, one richer and more meaningful than it might have been."

In a personal communication, Trisha Meili told me that a return to running was a significant contributor to her cognitive recovery. In 1995 she would complete the New York City Marathon in a time of 4:31. "Not

too bad!" she wrote in a recent e-mail. Not too bad indeed! So, too, has been her work in inspiring others
who have suffered similar injuries. Some of that work

Trisha Meili at the Hope and Possibility Run,
Central Park, 2007.

began with a published study where she was both a participant and one of the study's authors.

It was research that examined the exercise habits of 240 individuals with traumatic brain injury, comparing the exercisers with the non-exercisers. Those who were active exercisers had fewer overall complaints and symptoms compared with the non-exercisers who, in turn, complained of more cognitive symptoms, suggesting that exercise may improve otherwise diminished cognitive faculties. Also, the exercisers were less depressed. This may indicate a linkage between the emotional and the intellectual.

The real limitation of the study was that it was retrospective, depending on past history, past memories, without allowing for other confounding factors that may have determined whether a person chooses to exercise or not. But since then, there have been better studies hinting at the value of exercise in the rehabilitation of people with brain damage from any cause.

Scientists have used sophisticated techniques to measure blood flow to the brain during rest and during exercise. The areas where blood flow seems to seek out and predominate are the hippocampus and its dentate nucleus. They, in turn, are part of the cerebrum. The cerebrum regulates specialized functions such as memory, orientation, perception and judgment, reasoning and thinking. These are the cognitive processes. Their geographic location corresponds to where the teacher says, "Put on your thinking cap." Before describing the studies, a brief orientation to the brain is in order.

The brain, unlike other organs such as skin, was always thought to be unable to repair itself, unable to regenerate tissue. Such a conclusion has now been overturned. The area where new memories are laid down, the dentate nucleus, is the region where brain tissue regeneration occurs. The phenomenon of tissue regeneration is termed neurogenesis.

To better understand some of the underlying mechanisms, a brief bit of neuroanatomy now may help. The cerebrum or "thinking cap" consists of rounded bundles or lobes. There is the frontal lobe, which, true to its name, is in the front of the head. Just below it, on both sides, are the temporal lobes. They reside at the level of the temples.

The hippocampus is a region in the lower portion of the temporal lobe of the cerebrum. The name derives from its shape, similar to that of a mythological creature. Its dentate nucleus is embedded in it. It is called dentate because of its tooth-like projections. A nucleus is like a hub, a series of interconnected nerve cells and their fibers (axons). The hippocampus, through its dentate nucleus, is concerned with basic drives, emotions, and the formation of recent memories.

You can liken these higher centers—particularly the dentate nucleus—to a finely tuned Stradivarius violin, delicate and sensitive to changes in climate, humidity,

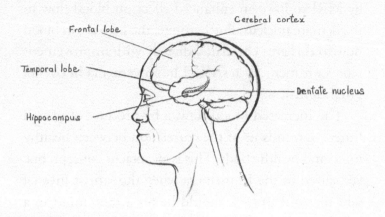

and human tinkering. You can say, too, that the cerebrum, along with its dentate nucleus subregion, is a high-maintenance complex. The dentate nucleus, a center sensitive to any of the subtle and not-so-subtle circulatory changes that come with aging, is particularly susceptible to damage and destruction.

Now some of the findings that will help explain Trisha Meili's remarkable recovery. In one part of an experiment, exercising animals were determined to have larger blood flow to the dentate nucleus. This increased blood volume coincided with increased findings of neurogenesis.

In the next part of that experiment, eleven exercising humans were instructed to exercise three hours a week for three months. Memory tests were administered at the onset of their exercise regimens. Exercise in the eleven humans, as in the animals, was also found by MRI to have an enhanced effect on blood flow to the dentate nucleus. Furthermore, the increase in blood flow to this area correlated directly with improvement scores on memory tests and improvements in overall physical fitness.

The increased blood flow, a by-product of overall fitness, reminds us of the correlation between healthy mind and healthy body. This is an ancient concept, one verbalized in the Roman era when the satirist Juvenal said that our prayers should be for a sane mind in a healthy body (*mens sana in corpore sano*).

Another study linking heart and blood (cardiovascular) fitness to fitness of brain tissue was conducted in 2006 at the University of Illinois. Here, fifty-nine otherwise healthy but sedentary volunteers, ages sixty through seventy-nine, were randomly assigned to aerobic training or to toning and stretching. For comparison purposes, twenty young adults underwent MRI's, otherwise not participating in the study. Both groups also had MRIs of their brains taken at the beginning and end of the six-month study.

Significant increases in brain volume of the cells and tracts in the brain were found only in the older adults who participated in the aerobic fitness training.

You can conclude again that fit body equals fit mind. As a result of physical fitness, you can expect to find the heart pumping larger quantities of blood to the brain, the areas that need the "high-octane fuel," specifically the areas that control memory and also link to the brain's emotional centers. With these enhanced volumes of blood come the essential fertilizers—oxygen and blood sugar (glucose).

A study from Finland observed that the rates of dementia and Alzheimer's disease among regularly active persons were less than half those among inactive persons. This hints at the promising role for exercise: A vigorous lifestyle may either prevent or retard the dementia of Alzheimer's disease.

Short-term memory losses, furthermore, often are the first sign heralding Alzheimer's disease. The first structural breakdown is often in the sensitive dentate nucleus of the hippocampus.

Another culprit terrorizing the dentate nucleus is type 2 diabetes mellitus. The onset of this malady is usually in middle or later life. Here the blood sugar (glucose) vital to brain function has difficulty getting into tissues and cells.

Studies on humans found that the higher the blood sugar level, the lower the test results for total recall. In other words, where the utilization of blood sugar—the fuel for intellectual function—was impaired, mental functioning was correspondingly impaired. Vigorous exercise, on the other hand, enhances the transport of blood sugar into the cells and tissues.

Trisha Meili's book has a subtitle saying it is a story of "Hope and Possibility." So, given the story of her life and the above studies, here are some possibilities.

Whatever can be done to benefit the circulation to the aging hippocampus region of the brain might slow the progression of the various degenerative processes—such as Alzheimer's disease—that assail the aging brain. Similarly, whatever that can be done to utilize blood glucose—the brain's principal nutrient—would benefit the hippocampus with its function of recent memory processes.

Enter now vigorous exercise with its known ability to enhance blood flow to the brain and with its known ability to lower blood glucose. Exercise, before the discovery of insulin, was a known treatment for children thought to be pre-diabetic. Exercise encourages glucose utilization in bodily tissues, cells, and organs. Vigorous exercise also increases blood volume and enhances blood flow, carrying with it its vital nutrients of oxygen and glucose to the brain.

Exercise, in a sense, becomes the Viagra of the brain—particularly the aging brain—restoring failing cognitive functions.

Years later, Dr. Robert S. Kurtz told Trisha Meili how amazing it was that her heart was still pumping away. Part of the reason was that she was in "... excellent athletic condition—and you're an indomitable person. You were in a situation where other people like you might well be dead—and you weren't."

Indomitable. Thus is introduced another intangible but no less real element. That element is the human spirit. Neurologist Dr. Roger Bannister, the first man to break the four-minute-mile barrier, penned, "No one can say you must not run faster than this or jump higher than that. The human spirit is indomitable."

The chapters that follow will be about people I have met along the way whose indomitable spirit will forever linger in memory.

NOTES

MRI (magnetic resonance imaging: This is an imaging technique that both visualizes and contrasts organs and tissues of the body by virtue of their magnetic fields. The magnetic fields are scanned and a computer-driven image is produced.

Dementia usually refers to deterioration of intellectual functions from any cause. Alzheimer's dementia is a specific form of dementia where there are abnormal forms of protein in aggregates forming plaques and tangles of nerves.

Achilles Track Club . . . For further information, go to: www.achillestrackclub.org

It was research that examined the exercise habits . . . . W. A. Gordon, M. Sliwinski, J. Echo, M. McLoughlin, M. Sheerer, T. E. Meili. The benefits of exercise in individuals with traumatic brain injury: a retrospective study; *J Trauma Rehabil* 1998; 13(4):58-67.

Scientists have used sophisticated techniques to measure blood flow to the brain during rest and during exercise. A. C. Pereira, D. E. Huddleston, A. M. Brickman, A. A. Sosunov, R. Hen, G. M. McKhann, R. Sloan, F. H. Gage, T. R. Brown, S. A. Small. An in vivo correlate of exercise-induced neurogenesis in the adult dentate gyrus. *Proc Natl Acad Sci USA* 2007;104:5638-5643.

The areas where blood flow seems to seek out and predominate are the hippocampus and its dentate nucleus. Ibid.

Hippocampus . . . For a comprehensive detailed description of the hippocampus and the dentate nucleus, go to www.psycheducation.org/emotion/hippocampus.htm. The title is: Memory, Learning, and Emotion: The Hippocampus.

Nucleus . . . A nucleus may be likened to a hub, in this instance a center consisting of interconnections of nerve cells and fibers.

In one part of an experiment, ... Pereira, et al. An in vivo correlate.

Another study linking heart . . . Stanley J. Colcombe, Kirk I. Erickson, Paige E. Scalf, Jenny S. Kim, Ruchika Prakash, Edward McAuley, Steriani Elavsky, David X. Marquez, Liang Hu and Arthur F. Kramer. Aerobic exercise training increases brain volume in aging humans. *J Geront: Biol Sci* 2006; 61:1166-70 (2006)

A study from Finland . . . S. Rovio, I. Kareholt, E.L. Helkala, M. Vilanen, H. Winblad, J. Tuomilehto, H. Soinen, A. Nissinen, and M. Kivipelto. Leisure-time physical activity at midlife and the risk of dementia and Alzheimer's disease. *Lancet Neurol* 2005; 4:705-11.

A vigorous lifestyle . . . W. Wu, A. M. Brickman, J. Luchsinger, P. Ferrazzano, P. Pichiule, M. Yoshita, T. Brown, C.

DeCarli, C. A. Barnes, R. Mayeux, S. J. Vannucci, S. A. Small. The brain in the age of old: the hippocampal formation is targeted differentially by diseases of late life. *Ann Neurol* December 2008; 64(6):698-706.

The first structural breakdown . . . . Ibid.

Studies on humans found that the higher the blood sugar level the lower the test results for total recall. Ibid.

No one can say you must . . . Bannister R. *The Four-Minute Mile.* New York: Lyons and Burford, 1994.

PART II

EXERCISE BRIDGES TO THE SPIRITUAL

In the 1950s, Dr. Jeremy Morris studied the London double-decker bus drivers and ticket takers. He found a lesser incidence of heart disease among the ticket takers, whose work required going up and down stairs as compared with the all-day-seated sedentary drivers. He and his friend and colleague Dr. Ralph Paffenbarger continued research over the years, documenting the benefits of exercise for a host of illnesses.

In an obituary telling of his life, Morris, having died in October 2009, only half a year away from his hundredth birthday, was quoted: "Exercise," he declared, "normalizes the workings of the body."

He was in effect saying that we were meant to be active, that exercise mobilizes our body's resources for the test ahead. We become mentally keener; our hearts beat more efficiently; neurohormones designed to elevate our mood and fine-tune our thinking are activated. We become the best we can be in body, mind, and spirit.

Spirit? Spirit, in the ordinary sense of the word, refers to an enthusiasm, a vital force, and an energy for living. Spiritual, again in the everyday sense of the word, refers to a concern for and sensitivity to the higher, more refined, abstract, and nonmaterial things in life.

You can find the marriage of the spirit and the spiritual in the essay "Cell Fever." In this story, a spirited college student embarks on a solitary winter run in the Connecticut woods. After a while his senses become acutely aware of his surroundings. His thoughts wander, then organize and crystallize as certain realizations dawn on him.

This phenomenon of awareness and sensitivity is believed to come about through a dominance reached by the right brain, our creative and abstract center. The apparent monotony of the run seems to stifle the logical side of the brain that believes only what we see and hear, rather than what our imaginative side is trying to tell us.

But enough of science. Scientific explanations take the fun out of this adventure, in the end trivializing the phenomenon. Without any further explanation of why, read about Tommy Williams who refused to allow multiple sclerosis to conquer his spirit, or Bill Lloyd who didn't let cancer interfere with his quest to give, or Glenn Cunningham whose spirit and philosophy of life enaled him to overcome burned legs and become a world-record holder in track.

Read about Dave Worthen, dying with Lou Gehrig's disease, vowing "denial to the strength sapping saprophytes of depression, despair, frustration, and fear." Read about George Sheehan's race with death to finish a manuscript that told of his journey to life's end, of Austin Newman who continued to compete in the pool and on the track at age ninety-three because "we're here." Read about Ralph Paffenbarger's relentless quest to research the benefits of exercise despite his crippling heart disease.

Read about the spirit needed for a city to survive. Or about a city boy, Irv Taylor, who found meaning within the early running scene, and departed when it became too modern, too commercial.

Just as this section began with the marriage of the spirit with the spiritual, it ends with a similar theme. Read about our relay team that swam the twenty-four-mile span of Tampa Bay. We did it to raise money for research into and public awareness of bipolar disorder. At race end, a relay member, the father of a boy who became victim of the disorder, pens an imagined letter to his departed son.

These are my heroes, people (and dogs) whose lifestyle of vigorous exercise was metaphor for the lives they led.

CELL FEVER

(1981 essay by Dr. Charles Kiell,
then a senior at Connecticut College)

One of the most important biological concepts is the cell theory, proposed by Schleiden and Schwann in the mid-19th century. It states that all life forms, from the amoeba to man and the great apes, are made of cells. Although the type and quantity of each cell varies with each genus and species, this theory nevertheless established man's common ground with the fish, spiders and trees: we are all composed of cellular building blocks. Modern biologists now play with individual genes and chromosomes, but they nevertheless know that the cell is still the smallest unit capable of sustaining life.

As zoology major, I find that my mind is often focused on cells. Sometimes, they frustrate me with their smallness and complications, but mostly, they fascinate me. Whether it is their marvelous inner architecture— the membranous canals called the endoplasmic reticulum, the pinocytotic vesicles that engulf extracellular objects—or their incredible ability to grow and reproduce, they still leave me in awe.

Cells, though, are sometimes too much on my mind. One afternoon's lab left my head swimming with them. I walked outside and for a moment my perceptions failed to register—or was it that they were suddenly registering with an unusual clarity? In the hazy light of the late afternoon, I was not seeking a park full of hurrying people, but a mass of minuscule messengers darting to and fro within the giant cell of the city, carrying out cellular functions.

When my overwrought brain needs fresh oxygen, I turn to running. Running has been a passion of mine for the past nine years. Sure, there is a running "boom" going on these days, but I've always thought of myself as one of the originals, one of those weirdos who used to lope around the streets in baggy gray sweatsuits. Those were the days before sweatsuits cost $80. Now, the roads sometimes look like racks from a fashionable sporting goods store, so numerous are the "True Believers" in their bright apparel. But I hardly ever run on the roads anymore.

I prefer to go off to the woods these days. There, things are different: on the run, I can sing a little song, do a little dance, and only the birds and trees will see. They don't care though. They grow, fly, blossom, flower, and I run. Sometimes, I'll be out running, my arms swinging loosely, my foot-plant solid, thighs pushing off strongly, and I think, "Fine, everything is smooth, just fine."

I feel this way today while running through a field behind Bloomingdale Road. The sun is getting low, and its orange color is increasing in intensity, but there is still an hour before sunset. No, I don't see the world in a wildflower, or the struggles of man embodied in the ephemera, but it is still beautiful. Yes, quite nice, I feel an urge to raise up my arms and shout, but I resist. Not that I'm overly inhibited—rather, to do so implies being superior, victorious, powerful, and I feel hardly such. Instead, I feel vastly mediocre, almost an intruder.

I think of the wood frogs and their mating calls, all done by instinct. For them, sociability comes naturally, no problem. For me, socializing is awkward, difficult, and unnatural. I must rely on whatever wit and quick thinking I have, and not on something inborn. Maybe I should ask Mr. Frog for a few lessons.

Over the past year or so, my goal while running has been to blend into the scenery, to flow along the landscape, to make it as effortless as possible. And during this run, I do kind of roll along, feel a kind of gentle push as I go up the little hill. But something else happens. As I look above the trees, I notice something I haven't seen before: there is a delimiting boundary—a membrane that surrounds my surroundings, the plasmalemma of a cell. The winding trail that I run along is something I've seen before under a microscope: the endoplasmic reticulum, one of those membranous intracellular roadways transporting compounds synthesized by the cell. These are not just rocks along the trail, but the protein-synthesizing ribosomes that line the inner surface of the endoplasmic reticulum. These are not just trees, but microfilaments and tonofibrils, the tubular structures that provide a skeleton for the cell.

So here I am, a solitary runner, coursing through the inner channels of something that is both smaller and larger than I am. Am I a messenger of RNA? Or in view of my greater resemblance to my mother, a molecule of transfer RNA?

Down the Thames I go, but it is no longer the

Thames; it is a massive capillary providing nourishment for the cell. (In fact, the river does provide water for some of the industrial plants there.) Then it's up the hill, back toward the college. The endoplasmic reticulum winds its way along the periphery of the cell; soon I see the roadway, and suddenly the endoplasmic reticulum becomes merely a trail again; the cell is now only a wood. I've been expelled from the cell. I wonder whether it will take me back. The trail winds away from the road, and then some marvelous pinocytotic vesicle reaches out and engulfs me; again, I am part of the cell, the trail again perceived to be an endoplasmic reticulum. I know now that I am an integral part of the cell's functioning, a part of the woods, and now understand what Walt Whitman meant when he wrote:

> The substantial words are in
> The earth and sea:
> They are in you.

Both the cell and I have moved together, functioned as one, no longer recognizing differences. I am now the earth and sea; the earth and sea are now me.

The run is now a memory; the mud on my shoes has long since dried. Sure, a lot of imagery was conjured up out there. But maybe, maybe it wasn't all worthless imagination. In our dealings and in our dependence on one another, don't we form one big community, one concerted mass of functioning protoplasm? I feel as did Casy, Steinbeck's itinerant preacher in *Grapes of Wrath*, who went into the wilderness to find his soul, but saw that he had none—only that he had a little piece of a great big soul. The woods across the road, the woods I saw as vast encompassing cell, now becomes one infinitely small part of a whole.

TOMMY WILLIAMS

Victor Altshul's description of our flying fantasies ("a more active experience [where] one feels almost magically free of ordinary bodily constraints) struck a note of remembrance when at my fortieth high school reunion, I met Tommy Williams, co-captain of our 1948 high school cross-country team.

As ad hoc treasurer for the event, a few months earlier, notice of his acceptance had come addressed to me. My elation over hearing from him was tempered by one disquieting note, his answer on the prepared questionnaire to occupation—"Policeman, medically retired." So it was a cruel case of poetic injustice when at one of the reunion tables I spotted Tommy in a wheelchair.

"Multiple sclerosis," his wife confided. He'd had it since 1973 and the last six years were in the wheelchair. But visiting with Tommy, if you didn't see the wheelchair, you'd notice little change. He was the same wisecracking, feisty outgoing guy. Still thin, though some of it was no doubt muscular wasting, he kidded his beefier classmates.

I reminded him of a precious memory in which he was a leading player. It was late in the cross-country season, 1948, just before the state meet when I sensed myself sharpening and nearing a peak. I had needled him all week, boasting that I would beat him in the big meet. In the race itself, I did come to a point where I was "flying," feet barely touching the ground as I passed other runners. On the cinder track into the last quarter mile, I heard Tommy behind me, grunting and straining, but I managed to hold on and come in ahead of him.

He didn't speak to me for the whole next week, not until the last meet of the year, the Eastern Interscholastic, when everything came back to normal and he finished a good twenty runners ahead of me. After that he must have forgiven my effrontery, and later he did write something nice in my yearbook.

Never before or after have I had that feeling of flying, but it happened then and to this day I live it time and again, in dreams and in fantasies. It was, for me, the "perfect race." But Tommy had no recollection of our dueling. As we filled in the years with each other—marriage, children, work—I learned that he had spent four years in the U.S. Air Force and had been in Korea. He had risen in the ranks of the Newark Police Force. "He was a good policeman," his wife told me.

Earlier, as I said, she had told me of the biological event, the disease, but Tommy told me of his illness. Not in words, but in spirit, a spirit that was unbroken. The reunion was an event he wouldn't miss. He had come to enjoy himself. He would later say how thrilled he was with the warmth and friendliness of the day.

Many of us hadn't seen one another—just as I hadn't seen Tommy—for at least forty years. As classmates, we shared something truly unique. Born in the Depression and living through war years, we had a closeness that bridged color and class. Many worked after school. Many walked together to school. Busing was unknown. Tommy was an amalgam of that spirit, that certain toughness and resiliency and sense of humor, that certain *something* we all had to varying degrees, but which the black man of his day needed to survive and to succeed, that something that in Tommy was still undiminished.

My dear friend Joe Boodin would feel something that day. His parents had worked in their grocery store sixteen hours a day, seven days a week, driven by their dream of educating their two sons who would later become physicians. Joe would help out in the store after school. He'd meet friends there. He'd eat there. Their home, a small apartment nearby, was only a place to sleep. Joe confessed to us that he never brought anyone home in all his four years of high school. Home was my house, another friend's house, the store, the school. Joe made an elegant speech this day and told about those things and said how today he had come home.

It was coming home, too, for Tommy. We gave out mock diplomas. As his high school picture flashed on a screen, and in the background Mendelssohn' s War March of the Priests played, he raced up in his wheelchair, arms thrown open wide, face beaming, proudly taking his "diploma." Our cross-country co-captain

Paul Kiell

Tommy Williams, Co-Capt.

had accepted disease but had rejected illness. If running is, as Donald Porter once wrote, "coming home to who we are," the old runner had come home this day. We all had come home.

Tommy Williams was part of my flying fantasy, the stuff dreams and fantasies are made of. That, graced by his spirit—a spirit competing with illness—will always be with me. Even if we don't meet again for another forty years.

Epilogue: Tommy would come to our forty-fifth and our fiftieth reunions and a few mini-reunions to follow. He died in 2002 at age seventy-one.

BILL LLOYD

"I'm going to run with Bill Lloyd." If you said this at the summer Monday night Lake Takanassee road races—with a shrug of the shoulders, a wink of the eye, a forced nonchalance—it was a sort of shorthand way of admitting that you had run out of alibis, felt less than ready to compete with your fellow runners, and preferred the anonymity of running way back in the pack with Bill Lloyd.

With Bill you were sure of two things: One was that he'd finish, the other was that he'd finish last. For keeping Bill company, though, your reward was a compelling lesson in how to give your all, because that was the only way Bill knew how to do things.

Bill had been with the original Shore Athletic Club, in the 1930s, doing weight lifting and bodybuilding, and then in 1963—long before any of us—he began running.

I first met him at the lake in 1971: Instant kindred spirits, we had noticed each other's gray hair. Later, I'm proud to say, we became friends. It's easy, you must realize, to know a runner. Just run with them a few times and you know the essentials of the person.

At first, though, because of the narrow stereotype I

then harbored, I found it hard to believe he was a lawyer. Lawyers, after all, aren't supposed to be soft-spoken, gentle, selfless, as Bill was. But then again, lawyers are tough, stubborn, tenacious, as Bill also was. (I saw that displayed in the no-nonsense manner in which he once handled, gratis, a legal matter for me.) He saw things through; he was a finisher. At Takanassee, it was axiomatic that the race wasn't over until Bill finished.

What do I remember about Bill Lloyd? I remember Labor Day 1972, going with a group to a ten-miler in Westport, Connecticut. In the trunk of the Lloyds' car were dozens of wrapped sandwiches and cases of beer and soda that Eileen and Bill had brought for all of us.

I remember Bill, standing at the bleakest post possible, somewhere along the Shore Marathon route one cold January day, handing out drinks and encouragement to the marathoners. It was a day that we ran over packed snow and before Bill or the other volunteers could pour it, the water would freeze in the containers. I remember thinking how much easier it was for me than for him, even though I'd run twenty-six miles that day. Bill would later get home with hands that had become numb and discolored. I didn't know it until years later, but Bill was right then in the midst of getting chemotherapy treatments; he had been advised to stay home. But he was out there. "They need me," he had told Eileen.

Besides the chemotherapy, he had undergone two

series of cobalt treatments. The side effects of these treatments are often worse than the illness itself. Once, after fifty-two cobalt treatments, his doctor told him he could again work; Bill told his doctor he'd never stopped working. Never lost a day. If ever you'd ask him how he felt, invariably he'd say he felt fine. If he felt bad—and he must have—no one ever knew.

Slowed by illness, Bill did less and less competitive running, and I saw little of him over the next few years. But before that, maybe three decades of summers now gone by, on a memorable evening in late August, I ran with Bill Lloyd.

It was handicap night and the 3.4-mile race was the evening's last event. Bill and I started about the same time, each of us given generous head starts, so much so I even had visions of winning.

But my dream soon went aglimmering, and before long I was in the back of the pack with Bill, as other runners and time just seemed to glide by us. Soon we were all alone. Bill didn't seem to notice or care.

Bill obviously was also less concerned with the tempo of modern living. Bill, I think, heard the music of the Renaissance man, of the Mozart symphony—steady, rhythmic, upbeat—proclaiming and celebrating the dignity of man.

When at last we got to the finish line, it was shrouded in semi-darkness. The days had been getting shorter. Almost everyone had gone home.

Before stepping over the line, I motioned for Bill to

precede me, but he'd have none of my offer. Last place had been his traditional responsibility. I had no choice but to finish before him. A moment later, he stepped over. The race was finished.

On May 28, 1982, Bill died. He was sixty-two. He left three daughters, all married, and five grandchildren. Eileen and Bill had been married for thirty-four years.

He had touched the lives of many people. They came to say good-bye at Saint Anne's Church in Keansburg, whose ample space could not accommodate the throng that spilled over into the streets.

Three fire trucks carried the flowers, and firemen in uniform came; Bill had been a volunteer fireman. Boy Scouts in uniform came; Bill used to devote half a day each week to scouts interested in learning the fundamentals of government and civics. Members of the First Aid Squad came; Bill had once been one of them. Little League youngsters and their parents came; Bill had donated his legal services to them. Members of other churches in town came; Bill had given his help to them, too. From the town council on which he served, from the Veterans of the American Legion, the Knights of Columbus—they all came. His brother Vincent, a priest, gave the eulogy. Summing it up, he said that Bill was a humble man.

So, how then do I remember him?

I remember most the time I ran with Bill Lloyd. I can still see the scene of two solitary figures, etched in the dusk of a long-ago late-summer evening, and in that fading twilight one of them puts his hand on the other's shoulder, gently nudging him ahead. That's how I remember Bill, always extending himself, always giving.

GLENN CUNNINGHAM

Whenever I think of Glenn Cunningham, I picture a tall, raw boned man. That image is fortified by early snapshots of him. He seems to tower over anyone else in the photo. If you didn't know better, you'd swear it was a young Gary Cooper, with that same lanky look, same dimpled grin. Look at archival films of Cunningham racing, and again he is tall. Look at the 1988 video of him running with the other old-timers at Madison Square Garden. Once more it is that tall man.

For the record: Glenn Cunningham was five-foot-nine. Years ago he was in a serious car accident and sustained severe neck injuries. That, coupled with the normal aging process, had to shrink him a few inches. So why do I remember that man who'd turn his whole body to face you so that he could look right at you the only way he knew to speak with someone—as being tall?

In the one picture I have of myself with him, we are the same height, and I was never taller than five-foot-eight. Once (when he was seven years old), by no stretch of the imagination could he have appeared tall. Maybe noble. Certainly brave, but not tall. No one can look tall when you're horizontal and bedridden; in young Glenn's case it was for several long months, with extensive burns, burns courtesy of a schoolhouse fire. His older brother Floyd, with him at the fire, would die nine days later from his wounds. Glenn's burns were so severe that doctors predicted he might never walk again. They had also warned that should infection set in, amputation was likely. And when some time passed, and the young Kansan farm boy's nostrils were assailed by the odor of decay and infection, he confided his deep fear to his father that now he would lose his legs. His dad instilled in him the frontier wisdom and philosophy that would later be singular to Glenn Cunningham: "Doctors," father told son, "they ain't always right."

That's how it was with Glenn Cunningham. He didn't know some things were impossible, so he went right ahead and got the job done. Once out of bed he devised his own homemade physical therapy. He would grab on to an old swinging gate for balance and then run. Or he would grab the tail of a mule and walk or run behind the animal. Ultimately he would set world records for distances of a half-mile to two miles, and run in two Olympic games, taking second place in the 1500m run at the 1936 Olympics. All of this despite burned and scarred legs, despite impaired circulation, despite weak transverse arches, and despite testing poorly on the endurance equipment of his day. Cunningham somehow had learned to go beyond himself.

At the post-Boston Marathon banquet of 1987 he told a group of running physicians that he wasn't really

Glenn Cunningham (746) on his way to a silver medal
the 1936 Olympic 1500m.

the fastest runner; rather what he had was enthusiasm. "It isn't the size of the bee," he said, "it's the enthusiasm with which the bee stings you that counts."

After his track career, and after serving in the U.S. Navy in the Second World War, he and his wife Ruth turned their time, their energies, and their financial resources, toward helping children from troubled homes. (He earned a living of sorts giving inspirational talks to young people. He had a distinct distaste for any nine-to-five job.)

From a chapter in *Crime in the Suburbs* by David Loth (1964), the following description is given:

> Along a dirt road outside Wichita, a tall, lean, long legged man is turning into the gap in a slightly dilapidated fence behind a sign that reads 'Wild Animal Farm.' He has just met a 'bad boy' sent to him by a juvenile court judge

in Baltimore. The tall man moves with a dancer's grace and his deep melodious voice puts quotation marks around 'bad boy' because he doesn't believe any such creature exists. If you spend time with him, he will almost convince you he is right. He is Glenn Cunningham, who more than thirty years ago ran the fastest mile in the world and has kept up an even faster pace ever since to snatch some 8,000 children—he figures—from all sorts of trouble, children who were disturbed, abandoned, abused, neglected or delinquent.

Again, it is that "tall man." The label of a "bad boy" or a "bad girl" he rejected out of hand. "I never met a 'bad boy,' I never met a 'bad girl.' I've never seen a child I didn't love," he had told the assembled post-marathon runner/doctors of that 1987 American Medical Athletic Association banquet.

He conceded we all do some bad things, and he would make a point of telling youngsters that he'd done a few bad things himself. He taught them well, taught the simple old-fashioned values: You told the truth, you worked hard, you didn't smoke, you didn't take drugs. Boy-girl relationships were out, but he had little problem with that—by the end of the day's chores on their 850-acre farm, the kids were too tired for anything else.

Though basic and simple, his ideas were ahead of his time. He espoused animal therapy. He would purchase animals for the children (deer, kangaroos, African mountain sheep, llamas, Brahmin cattle donkeys, saddle horses, pinto ponies), and each youngster would be given one of them to care for. "An animal is absolutely honest," he pointed out. "It will respond to love and kindness, will give its trust to someone who earns it, and kick the devil out of someone who doesn't . . . a kid will respond deeply to an animal when he won't respond to anyone else."

Their work, by the way, was financed internally. (Fiercely independent as he was, I suspect Cunningham didn't encourage outside contributions, avoiding external control of any kind.) From his lectures and talks he did generate a bit of income, and possibly some money was raised from the livestock and the farm itself, but never money to make ends meet considering their twelve children plus the children they were caring for, to say nothing of the veritable zoo of animals that had to be fed. They received little outside financial help.

Finally, unable to pay even the interest on the debt accrued, Ruth and Glenn Cunningham had to leave their work behind. Journalists writing about his financial plight at the time spoke of his sanguine outlook. Once, in New York, he had in his pocket his life's savings, $18, yet he considered himself the richest man in the world. His greatest race, he said, was still ahead of him—the work with the troubled kids he and Ruth had dedicated themselves to. All he wanted, though, was the opportunity to give his lectures and talks so that he could continue to finance his work.

Before Cunningham visited us in Boston in 1987,

I had done a telephone interview with him. I'd never forget how he said that the greatest inspiration in his life was his parents, pioneer people who never knew defeat. And for our banquet he had eschewed an honorarium, asking only that he could bring his wife along.

Memories filtered back to me when recently I put my hand in the pocket of the suit I wore the night of that banquet. There I came upon the notes I had prepared so that I could properly introduce a boyhood idol, a man who held countless records, a man whose name you'd mention along with Babe Ruth, Bill Tilden, a man who would tell us that he never met a bad boy, never met a bad girl, never saw a child he didn't love, a man who would tell us that the only way to elevate yourself was to bend down to help someone else.

No wonder I was looking up at him as I felt my hand engulfed by the catcher's mitt that was his right hand. Tall? He was more than tall. He was a giant.

Later, as we were leaving the banquet area, I asked him to please stop calling me doctor. He reluctantly agreed to cease and desist only when I threatened to call him the same thing. Cunningham, you might know, had earned a Ph.D. in biological sciences at New York University.

We corresponded over the next year. He wrote how he was looking forward to being with all of us again at that April seminar. Six weeks before it, the tall man would die. He was seventy-eight years old.

Glenn Cunningham had held records from the half mile to the two-mile event. In his day, whenever they were broken, it was usually he who did the breaking. Today, none of his track records stand. But he has one record that will never be broken. He was surely the tallest five-foot-nine man who ever lived.

DAVID WORTHEN

"David was a doctor before he was a runner."

So remarked chief medical director Dr. John Gronvall on June 18, 1987, in the Committee Room for Veteran's Affairs. He was speaking before a gathering of several hundred, of family, friends, and colleagues, distinguished U.S. congressmen, senators, and the surgeon general. They were all there to honor David Worthen, M.D., Assistant Chief Medical Director for Academic Affairs, Veterans' Administration, Washington, D.C. Dave, you see, was reluctantly stepping aside. The clinical symptoms were all too apparent, the diagnosis had been established.

I was there. For me, the evening was filled with a certain touch of déja-vu. My thoughts would wander back, near half a century ago, to the time my friend Allen Berlin and I were sitting in that old movie house, transfixed, passing a bag of peanuts between us as we watched the scene in *Pride of the Yankees*.

There, a stricken Lou Gehrig, in a valedictory to life, tells a hushed and packed stadium that "today I consider myself the luckiest man on the face of the earth."

But now it was Dave who owned the illness given

dignity by the legendary first baseman, an illness sometimes called Lou Gehrig's disease, more commonly termed by the medical world as amyotrophic lateral sclerosis. And now, too, instead of a movie house, it was the House of Representatives (Canon Office Building), and instead of a bag of peanuts, in our hands all of us would grasp fine stem-glasses filled with champagne, raising them more than a few times to toast the scholarship, the courage, the leadership of the doctor-become-runner David Worthen.

A quote from Wayne Marsh, director of Glaucoma Service at the University of Oklahoma, was read: "Your contribution to the treatment of glaucoma has been unequaled by any investigator in this century. You're responsible for the initial development of the procedure known today as argon laser trabeculoplasty, which has become the leading surgical procedure in the treatment of glaucoma."

A letter was read from Theodor Seuss Geisel, author of the Dr. Seuss books. Geisel was also a beneficiary of Dave's care. In 1978 he had dedicated his book—*I Can See with My Eyes Shut*—to Dave: "Dear David, to me you will always be the Eye-Guy who goes far beyond his patient's eyes and fixes up his soul as well."

Jim Hahn had worked with Dave and wrote that "no matter how many hours you put in, he'll put in more, one always feels fat by comparison." That brought laughter, and despite the darkness hovering over the event, it told of a bright, uplifting evening.

The assistant chief director for academic affairs had taught his pupils well.

They remarked how it was Dave who had reassured and comforted his friends and colleagues. In an account of his illness, Dave's recent journal writing was quoted:

> I use my ingenuity to discover new ways of accomplishing activities as functions decline. I vowed denial to the strength sapping saprophytes of depression, despair, frustration, and fear. As ability is lost, there is no lessening of the will to bump against whatever can be done and achieve whatever can be achieved.

More stories were told; more quotes were proffered, more toasts given to Dave's courage, to his leadership, to his enthusiasm.

History, voiced in elegant prose and poignant quotes, flowed on. Ah, those quotes . . . There was such a profusion of them, one more eloquent than the other, that Dr. Gronvall was prompted to quip that you ran the risk of being accused of plagiarism when you borrowed from many people, but here it was "research."

My own research uncovered words of an earlier inhabitant of the D.C. area, who in 1901 wrote about the single trait in Dave that all of us less talented, all of us less thin by comparison, could emulate: It is *enthusiasm.* "Enthusiasm," wrote Woodrow Wilson, "sets the powers free."

David Worthen running the Boston Marathon, circa 1980.

That concept of freedom was echoed in Dave's favorite quote by another onetime local resident, Thomas Jefferson: "I have sworn upon the altar of God, eternal hostility against every form of tyranny over the mind of man." How strangely kind it is, then, that when a cruel illness fell on Dave, it was the one that spares the mind and the spirit.

Nearing the end of the evening, Dr. Gronvall would announce the establishment of the "David M. Worthen Award for Academic Excellence." Dave next gave his thanks:

It's an honor for me, and although my body is weakened and somewhat battered, I want you to know that inside, the soul, the spirit and the heart have a boundless energy and a boundless ambition and boundless love that I send to all of you. And I thank you for being here this night. Not only for me that we can share again all that we have done together but that my family, who sees me as just "that guy who goes to work in the morning in his running outfit" will know that what I do when I'm away from them has value and meaning to other people . . . There is no value I value higher than the freedom of the mind and the body and the spirit. And the combining of those values at this moment gives me great joy, and I hope that each of you will join in this moment of rejoicing. Thank you all, dear friends.

Ten months later, the runner-doctor would breathe no more. But before the inevitable, in published scientific articles, we can relish a few fruits born of his spirit.

For example, from the *Journal of the American Medical Association*, in his article titled "Inside the Diagnosis," he described how progressive handicap was a challenge to his ingenuity. He wrote, too, what a blessing it was to know the time of death, that this knowledge was a "gift" that "compensates for the slow dissolution of movement."

In another article for the *Annals of Sports Medicine*, he put himself in the third person and objectively described his illness, at the same time establishing a link between his recent electrical injury to his left arm and the onset of his ALS. He called his years of competition, conditioning, and excellent physical and emotional fitness, a "competitive edge" in managing the physical, emotional, and spiritual challenges of the disease.

When neurologist, runner, and first man to break the four-minute-mile Roger Bannister wrote of the indomitable human spirit, he must have been thinking of Dave Worthen. For after all, as they said in the classic movie story *Chariots of Fire*, "Life is a great race and what are we but runners."

Postscript: In the article that Dave wrote for the *Annals of Sports Medicine,* he had researched the literature and listed cases where trauma seemed to be a risk factor in the disorder. That was 1987; he died in 1988. Just now, August 2010, there was an announcement of a scientific article to be published in the September *Journal of Neuropathology and Experimental Neurology* showing possible links between an illness identical to ALS in athletes to their known history of head trauma. (When Worthen suffered the electrical injury he did experience a brief fainting spell.) Only time will tell, but Dave may have been on to something in his research linking ALS, or a form of it, to certain traumatic injuries.

GEORGE SHEEHAN

On pages of his best seller *Running and Being*, George Sheehan penned these lines:

> Only in another autumn, in another season in heaven, will I relive that finish. An impossible quarter-mile sprint and then holding on to the man I had just beaten so I wouldn't fall down. Hearing his heart pounding against my ear and my own beating in unison. Knowing only that and a world suddenly filled with friends saying nice things to an aging man who felt ageless in autumn.

I always like to tell the story of how I was a man, probably not *the* man, he once beat. For me it wasn't in autumn, rather it was summer, the summer of '71, in a 3.4-mile road race at Lake Takanassee. The run would go four times around the lake. Here it was that he overcame my three-minute handicap to edge me by a fraction of a second, simultaneously seizing third place and snatching along with it the medal I was instants before dreaming about. The local press took a picture of the first five of us in order of finish. The "Running Doctor" sent me that picture, still a precious memento, my welcome to the world of Dr. George Sheehan.

Now, more than two decades of autumns gone by,

it was back to Lake Takanassee—to that large bright red, imposing yet austere edifice, St. Michael's Church, sitting there at the northeast corner of the lake, with its high-rise marble altar and huge stained-glass windows, outlined against a flannel-gray sunless sky full with the damp chilly air. It was back to where it all began; a day you could say was good for runners.

In the last few years before he died, I'd hear George Sheehan ruminate over what would be his monument. What could he leave of lasting value? He had always played down his role as a parent, but his children had something else to say about that:

"Dad, I remember as a young girl," wrote Ann (not trusting their emotional control, the sons—no stalwarts themselves—spoke for their sisters), "you took me to track meets. I found the relay as the most exciting race. I knew the critical moment was the passing of the baton. You ran your legs like a champion. You ran hard and well. You put it way out in front. Because you faced your death so directly, you passed your baton to us gently and courageously so we wouldn't miss a step. Thanks Dad, I'll miss you."

"To my father," from Mary Jane: "Your death left your final gift to all of us. It was filled with your love and courage, your brilliant intellect and wonderful humor. It was your total offering. True to your philosophy, you gave it your all, fought the good fight, and truly went the distance with grace and bravery. You never let us know how hard the struggle was. 'My days are wonderful,' you said. 'I have family and friends, my book to work on, the ocean to contemplate.' You never told us what you must have felt—the pain, the frustration, and, ultimately, the loneliness of the dying process.

"Every family weekend was a party, with you the gracious host. You made our life with you such fun, that we were all in perpetual denial that you would have to leave us. At our last family vacation together in mid-September, at an ocean front home, you emerged one afternoon determined to take what you must have known was you last swim in your beloved ocean. I will never forget you then, your frail body battered by the waves, supported by your strong beautiful sons, their arms around you; you clung to them lovingly and you relished every moment. You were so brave. Those of us watching from the beach cried from the beauty of it all. One of the last days I had with you, we were alone. At one point in our conversation, I became emotional (unusual for me). I apologized, thinking it was upsetting you. Instead you smiled and said laughingly, 'Mary Jane, it is not worth going through all of this if people aren't going to cry about me.' So today, we will all cry for you, even as we celebrate your remarkable life. As your daughter, I want to tell you that I love and miss you already. My heart is breaking."

Peter, their son the doctor, not without a touch of humor, took the baton. His theme was courage, his father 's courage. But first he read lines from his sister Monica and with a subtle aside, corrected her writing: "It is this time with my father that has been a gift from God, a time that I will always be grateful for." ("for which I will always be grateful," Peter corrected.)

Peter continued, quoting Monica. Her words, in part, read: "My father was a child who had hurt me and then healed me.

"In him I found a father and friend and myself—both teacher and student until his last breath. 'Life is for the living. There are always more stories to tell and things to learn—that's where the real joy lies—in experience—in the ability to let life affect you in ways that you could never conceive.' This is what he gave me."

As a young boy Peter had asked his father about his experiences in the war. Heartened by hearing that his father had been in a battle Peter then asked: "What did you do during the battle?" Anticipating something heroic, he heard his father reply, 'I hid under a mattress.'"

"This was a guy who hadn't been to a dentist in thirty years," Peter quipped. But in the last year or more, "when the tumor finally advanced, we knew then the clock was ticking and he made this his final project, and his final project was to die. He read about death, he wrote about death, he ate, drank, slept, everything about death. Everything was death. His final project was to make his death easier for his family."

When the end did come, Peter described his feelings: "I went home. The next morning, I got the news. And my emotion was very curious, it was more awe and respect, and I thought, 'Oh my God, he did it, he did it, he accomplished it!' He died a graceful death. He reunited a family that had been torn over the years and he finished the book. I think his death was his final and perhaps his most rewarding achievement of his great life, and I can say that in the list of his many attributes, we can now add courage."

With "Sheehanesque" humor ("His greatest gift to me, I think," spoke son George, "was his sense of humor"), they alluded to his zest for life: "'If the upper case *I* breaks,'" Andrew Sheehan once told him, "'you'll have to throw that thing out.'"

This brought a big laugh from the assembled. Yet it was always his experience, his learning, his mistakes, his life . . . warts and all, that he was able to write about and so teach: In one of his last columns he wrote of his inability to find the words of the poet or the lyricist, but in its place the next best thing is "the recounting of personal experience . . . when you cannot express the human condition in poem or song or anecdotes, you can reveal it in yourself." "At the root of all writing," he said, "is the expression of a personality in evolution."

"My father was the luckiest man I knew over the last six months," wrote John Sheehan, "to see the love between my mother and him after forty-nine years of marriage. It brought tears to my eyes many a night driving home. That's why my brother is reading this for me." Earlier John gave his thanks: "I think I'm most thankful to my father for the things he didn't do: He was never demanding of me, he never discouraged me, he never doubted me, and, he didn't teach me how to tip."

Again laughter. Again the Sheehan humor. But here Sheehan had always given himself a bad rap, often saying how cheap he was. But he wasn't. He merely got his money's worth out of life. Like Thoreau, he sucked out life's essence.

Experience was the key word. Ann quoted him: "There is a world out there filled with interesting ideas and experiences. Find one that you love and run with it."

"Dad wanted to experience and live each day—not in the past, not in the future but in the present—and that was his gift to me," wrote Sara. "In the last week Dad wanted to hear my stories and experiences and as

I drove home each week, I reflected on my life and fashioned it into a wonderful story because that is what he taught me. He taught me how to live."

Michael wrote also about an autumn day twenty years earlier when he was a 110-pound freshman member of Red Bank Catholic's cross-country team: "With a short uphill distance to the finish and having conceded first place to another, I was locked in a battle for second. Giving my all, I still could not break away, but as we turned the corner for home, there you stood, out of nowhere, shouting 'Now Michael, take him on the hill!'

"And I did.

"The emotion of that day is still indescribable, and, as I told you years later, that was the day you became my father and I became your son. It had nothing to do with running—just for the pure experience of letting me learn on my own, knowing that around each corner, each threshold in life, you would be there. And it's still truly a peak experience every time I realize that you are, and always will be, a part of me."

Nora had a particular memory of her father. She wrote of it and more: "I remember a day at the Reds. The Reds was my father's family beach compound. I was swimming in the ocean and I had gone out too far. The waves were pulling me out, crashing on me, and I was terrified. Then I heard a voice calling to me, 'I am coming Nora,' you screamed, and I saw you tiny in the distance, swimming out to me to save me and I wasn't afraid. You always believed that I would do something special and your message was, 'Do what you love most. The Sheehans are late bloomers,' you would say, 'don't worry, you will find what you were meant to do . . .' During the years that you were gone, I tried to stay angry and shut you out. I thought I had lost you, that you were lost, but you came back and we met last year and you gave me your final gift that I had been waiting for, but had forgotten. You gave me your love and for that, you will always be inside me, cheering me on, protecting me."

The years that you were gone. Experience had its hurtful dimension. He wasn't spared the time he had left home to seek new experiences: "When you walked out on Mom, I was angry, but I didn't feel abandoned," Tim recounted. "You never went so far as you thought. You say you were so lucky to come back and find your family. But we were the lucky ones. You were the great champion of self, but you worked at becoming selfless. Always a good thief, you found a rabbi somewhere on the radio, somewhere on the highway, who gave you a definition of sin that met your terms. It was sufficiently ambitious, sufficiently challenging. 'Sin,' the rabbi said, was 'closing the circle of concern.'

"It was a high standard to keep that circle open and you worked wonderfully to attain it."

George III summed up. As he spoke, the chimes signaling midday were ringing out. A wedding scheduled for noon was being held up. "Backstage" (I was later told about this), the monsignor expressed his sense of urgency. "How can you stop these people," Father Brady, Irish brogue and all, pleaded, "when they're all out there spilling their guts out."

Upstage son George was speaking, quoting his father: "'Life is not a spectator sport, you get in the experience, you learn from it.' I remember later on he was writing, 'beware of the mob' to the runners at the beginning of the marathon. 'They are irrational.' He wanted you to stand on your own feet and learn your own lessons. When he went on the road he would often say, 'I am here to preach heresy, make the right choices, but do the homework.'"

His was a storied life, an epic life. He was the Pied Piper of a world he helped define and divine. The tune he piped out proclaimed that "the hero is you," that "when you are your best that is the real you," and to hear the myriad variations of these lyrics we followed him from Takanassee's quiet waters and gentle breezes to the brawling rises of Central Park and the potholes and decay of the Bronx and Harlem, to the undulating hills of Newton Lower Falls, to points west, all the way to the whispering waves lapping at the beaches of Waikiki. And now it was back to Takanassee where we could follow him no more.

The Irish bagpipes played the "going home" theme from a Dvorak symphony and I thought of George Sheehan telling us the story of how in some long ago Boston Marathon, at about the twenty-second mile, he could run not another step and told Nina Kuscsik to "Just take me home."

After the funeral his body was cremated. Some time later two trees were planted along the banks of the lake and his ashes were buried underneath. He was home, where running races are held and where runners can have impossible finishes and be the best they can be.

George Sheehan in a Takanassee road race.

AUSTIN NEWMAN

They wrote about him in the *Fastlane*—a local New Jersey swimming newsletter—saying:

An amazing athlete, Austin was a fixture in Master's Swimming. His many friends in the swimming community and beyond will sorely miss him.

Then they excerpted from the obituary in the local newspaper, the *Asbury Park Press*:

Austin Francis Newman, 93, of Toms River, passed away Monday, May 18, 2009. Mr. Newman was born November 21, 1915 in Elizabeth. He lived in Westfield for most of his adult life before moving to Toms River in 2001. He was employed by Elastic Stop Nut, Union (NJ) and retired in 1982.

Mr. Newman was known for his athletic accomplishments. In addition to his national and world records in swimming, he was inducted into the USA Track & Field Masters Hall of Fame in 2007 for his running prowess. His selection was based on his three national records, five world records, and 22 national championships as a middle distance runner. He was virtually unbeatable is his age group in numerous triathlons.

I have my own memories of Austin. If you look at the picture above, taken in May 1990, it shows Austin Newman edging me at the end of a fifteen-kilometer road race.

He was seventy-five at the time. I was fifteen years his junior. Although I remember him for that race, I remember him most for his grand spirit, his enthusiasm and zest for life. Above all, I remember him most for two simple words he once uttered.

It was 1996 and we were both competing at the YMCA Masters Swimming Nationals, that year held in Orlando. He had already turned eighty and would win all of his events for his age group. At about the second day of the four-day meet, in the midst of my establishing an age-group world record for nervous trips to the men's room, I inquired to all assembled the existential question: "Why do we do this if it makes us so uptight?"

Austin's riposte, as he shrugged his shoulders and turned his palms up, was . . . "We're here."

"We're here." To explain his words runs the peril of missing the mark, but I'll try to come close:

He said only two words, but his facial expression and his body language were proclaiming that life is not a spectator sport, that it is our responsibility to extend ourselves in everything we do, to do our best no matter what, that we owe it to our children and grandchildren and our friends to set an example.

That was 1996. Now it's 2005, fifteen years have passed since the road race where photographic history recorded his edging me out at race finish. Here I'm trying to break his New Jersey state record for the long-course 200-meter freestyle. If you could have superimposed our road-race finish on to his swim performance that very same year, he would have been ahead of me in the year 2005 by the same distance he had led me in the 1990 run photo.

I'll miss seeing Austin Newman at the meets, with his ready smile and strong handshake. Rest in peace old friend. Your records, your example, your person will never be matched.

RALPH PAFFENBARGER

The photo above shows Ralph Paffenbarger at the American College of Sports Medicine's fifty-fifth annual meeting in late 2006. His physical reserves depleted by illness, he still persevered and was able to make a significant contribution to that meeting. He would die in July 2007. His research on exercise has become the gold standard for exercise prescriptions.

Paff's careers in both athletics and medicine were marked by ultimates. A list of his athletic achievements includes 151 marathons and longer races. He ran the Boston Marathon twenty-two times and the New York City Marathon nine times, plus eight Western States 100-milers. The list of his scientific honors goes on for five typed pages; a list of his papers published in scientific journals, including the *New England Journal of Medicine*, the *Journal of the American Medical Association*, the *British Medical Journal*, and *Lancet*, goes on for twenty-four typed pages.

Along with his colleague and friend Dr. Jeremy Morris of Great Britain, he was awarded the 1996 International Olympic Committee (IOC) Prize. It is given every two years. It was for their research into links between physical activity and reduced risk of disease. Paff and Morris had collaborated for many years on a number of studies, including the ongoing College Alumni Health Study (CAHS), which began in 1960 and followed fifty-thousand college graduates throughout their lives.

The CAHS was the first major study to demonstrate to the satisfaction of even the most skeptical that if you are, or become, active, you lower your risk of a variety of ailments, including heart disease, hypertension, type 2 diabetes, some types of cancer, osteoporosis, and depression.

On October 6, 2007, at their Faculty Club, Stanford University hosted a memorial service for Ralph. Friends and colleagues came from all over the world to attend. His contributions were cited, and some of us commented about the person. Here are some of my spoken words that day:

"In speaking of Ralph's athletic years, one cannot sever those moments from his very essence, for they are but extensions, only metaphor, telling what he was made of. For me, he was a noble anachronism. He eschewed the instant gratifications of modern day. He valued only what he had earned through hard work, study, and discipline.

"No cable for his TV, he watched television only for the news, and only to supplement his reading of the *New York Times*. He never adjusted to using a computer or to digital instant picture taking; rather he preferred tinkering with an old Leica he had bought secondhand. He savored the growing of his own tomatoes and longed for the day he could once more listen to the radio sounds coming from the crystal set he might assemble.

"His life's ethic was manifest in his running. He was an ultramarathoner; the belt buckle he wore—and I doubt he ever took it off—was for traversing the 100-mile Transierra course in record time. In April 1988, he engaged in an adventurous, if not ludicrous, odyssey: On April 17, after completing the London Marathon, he reached Boston on April 18, just in time to run the BAA Marathon. A few days later he landed in New Jersey to lecture at a sports medicine seminar. Then on April 24 he ran the US Olympic Trials Marathon right in the shadow of Ellis Island.

"Here is what Peter Jokl, orthopedist and chief of the section of sports medicine at Yale University, said of him: 'Ralph was a great scientist but most importantly an honest and caring friend, a real mensch. He was one of the people that we all admired, especially my father.'

"Peter Jokl's late father, the esteemed Dr. Ernst Jokl, was also a scholar athlete. In his lectures on heart disease and exercise he would remark that the diseased heart was capable of extraordinary performance. Illustrating Jokl's observation, Ralph, shortly after running the 1990 Boston Marathon—irony of ironies—was found to have extensive heart disease. Still driven to making a difference in the lives of others, despite increasing infirmity over the years, he continued to exercise and engage in his research, contributed to countless scientific papers, lectures, and seminars on sports medicine. In 2003, for example, he was keynote speaker at an international sports medicine seminar in Finland.

"All the while his athletic capacities were waning. Yet he persevered in his desire to be helpful, to make a difference. Some of those ways were rather unique. For instance, undaunted by the monetary fines his wife JoAnn imposed on him for his backseat driving, virtually commanded into silence by her, he nevertheless persisted in helping JoAnn with negotiating the more difficult road turns: Summoning up his athleticism, simulating the hitter trying to steer his batted ball to the fair side of the foul line, Ralph would twist and gyrate his body in accord with the angle of the turn. Forgetting that association does not necessarily mean causation, Ralph must have felt he had made a positive contribution to her safe driving.

"I have fond memories, too, of the many times Joe Boodin and I would come to Berkeley and stay over a few nights. Along with JoAnn, we were an Alcatraz Triathlon team. We were the New Jersey Schleppers. I remember Ralph's expression of joy when I would reach shore on the swim; I remember the expression of love I saw on his face when JoAnn once gave an impromptu cello recital at their home. And I remember, too, his utter distress when I was shivering and shaking uncontrollably at one Alcatraz swim finish. He covered me with his coat. I became finally manageable only moments before he was about to cover me, literally, with the very shirt off his back.

"How do you sum up the life of a gentle man, a man who radiated so much dignity? He was a mensch: Like many Yiddish expressions, *mensch* is now in the dictionary. It refers to somebody good, kind, decent, and honorable. That is how we can all remember Ralph Paffenbarger. He was good, kind, decent, and honorable—a real mensch."

A CITY NEEDS SPIRIT TO SURVIVE

Coming back to run in the Newark (New Jersey) Distance Classic in 1984 gave an inveterate nostalgic like me just another excuse to make one of those melancholy visits to what was left of the old neighborhood.

Even though it would be unrecognizable—a veritable repository of squalor, neglect, and destruction—I was still drawn to that section of Newark just above where Clinton and Elizabeth Avenues meet, back to Milford Avenue.

Just hearing the name of the street, or seeing a burned-out, boarded-up apartment building, floods my mind with memories. Particularly poignant was the tail end of one sweltering summer in the early 1940s. Time hung heavy and we were forever running out of things to do. My friends and I looked forward to a trip to Olympic Park in Irvington, then boasting the world's largest freshwater pool, adventurous rides, and unlimited prizes for the skillful and the daring.

But our eagerly anticipated outing would never come to be. Apparently I had been sick with a "summer cold" a few weeks earlier and was judged by my mother to be insufficiently recovered.

My "resistance," she determined, was low, and an amusement park—which everyone then knew—was breeding ground for polio and other assorted ills, besides being the hangout for some rather undesirable types; it was certainly deemed as a not so wholesome place for me.

My purported dubious resistance created a bit of a stir on the block, reducing me to a sort of quasi-pariah, to be handled delicately and shunned whenever tactfully possible. But the matter would soon blow over, years would roll on, and all of us would move from the area. One by one, our houses would be leveled, my mother would die, Olympic Park would yield to an industrial park, and the block itself would all but disintegrate.

Although my "resistance" would wax and wane over the years and finally fade into obscurity, the whole concept of resistance was coming into vogue in the 1970s and '80s, part of the concept of stress, a concept everyone quotes but few understand. *Resistance* is one of the late Hans Selye's stages in his General Adaptation Syndrome—our response to any challenge or "stress."

The first stage of the General Adaptation Syndrome or the "alarm" stage is the calling up of resources. Blood is pumped to the arms and legs, blood pressure may rise, heart rate may quicken. We are mobilized for the demand; our "resistance" is being built. The trigger may be any type of challenge such as invading bacteria or virus, a competitive athletic event, an insult, or any threat into one's physical or psychic integrity. Once mobilized you are in the stage called "resistance." Alas for me, my resistance was calibrated to be insufficient for that Olympic Park excursion.

The stage after resistance, where the demand is too strong, where the combined resources of the being are overwhelmed, enters now the final stage called "exhaustion," characterized by injury to one's body or to one's ego, even death itself.

Such was the scene of my March 1984 return to the old neighborhood, seen even in earlier visits where I'd take my children on a pilgrimage to their father 's roots, from which weeds have now sprouted: weeds and wild-looking coarse shrubs, rocks, beer cans, broken whiskey bottles and discarded needles and syringes—the spoor of the wayfarer who sometimes aimlessly wanders through or meets with others at appointed hours to sell their contraband goods.

My children listen patiently, exchanging with one another that "We've-heard-it-before" look as I spin what they call my "war stories." They listen not without a bit of good-natured condescension and much incredulity when I tell them that the old tires strewn about, surrounded by that rusty, sagging chain fence, actually cover the ground where Mrs. Austin's tulips, gardenias, flowering shrubs, giant poplars and sprawling rosebushes once delighted the neighborhood and attracted garden lovers for miles around.

I tell them too, that on the corner where the heaped

rubble lies was the home and office of Dr. Stern, Max Stern, the "fight doctor." I tell them how we'd wait around outside to collect the autographs of a Tony Galento after his match with Joe Louis, of a Tippy Larkin or an Allie Stolz, and how once I was late in getting back to class at South Side High School after lunch because I waited in the crowd to see Tony Zale and Rocky Graziano emerge after the pre-fight physical for their 1948 championship bout in Ruppert Stadium (also gone).

It was impossible for me then to orient myself as to where our fig tree was, or the victory garden, or where Dr. Schacter's goldfish pond lay. And where was the cherry tree, that peach tree, and those grapevines crawling all over the backyard fences?

All were gone.

Across the street, facing what used to be my father's dental office, are the remains of No. 5 Milford Avenue, once a sturdy brick apartment building with stone lions in front. Its open windows bare burned-out black, and a few shards of glass resemble jagged broken teeth—a dentist's nightmare. This toothless leer was a mockingly macabre metaphor of Newark and the 1984 inner city. It is Selye's last stage of adaptation to stress, but it is stress in the breach, stress absented, the apathy born of drugs and alcohol.

"Freedom from stress," Selye said, "is death." Was the death a result of high stress and low resistance, or of resistance finally overwhelmed, thus leading to the

final absence of stress, a state that also destroyed the ancient great city of Rome? To try to explain causes here converts the dentist's nightmare into the nightmare of the social psychologist. Only the end stage was obvious.

But where one section of Newark bore the imprimatur of death, another would breathe life. On March 25 of that year, the city held its ninth annual Newark Distance Classic, originally the idea of then mayor Kenneth A. Gibson. This 20-kilometer (twelve-and-a-half-mile) run, like others of its kind, was a classic in that it expressed classic values: hard work, discipline, and sacrifice. They are both generated and expressed by the runner in training and in competition.

In training, the athlete enacts Selye's alarm and resistance stages, while at the same time avoiding the excesses and abuses from too much demand

—overtraining or exploitation of the body leading to the exhaustion phase.

The athlete trains by imposing incremental demands, actually calculated stresses on the body, to build up its endurance and strength, otherwise known as resistance. Athletic conditioning is really a process of breakdown and repair, the planned process of mild tissue breakdowns stimulating an overreaction of repair and regeneration.

In effect, the athlete enacts our inner instinctual struggle between life and death, love and aggression, creation and destruction.

But back to the city: The Romans expressed the dictum: *Ad astra per aspera* ("To the stars through struggle"). Selye, though, went beyond adaptation and beyond stress, and postulated an ultimate meaning to our struggle. He spoke of "intercellular altruism."

It begins with the competition of single cells to survive, followed by the formation of multicellular organisms and then the formation of colonies of more complex interacting cells no longer competing but interdependent.

Since the strength of the whole depends on the coordination of its parts, individual sacrifice and hard work are needed for the survival of the whole. This model of enlightened self-interest, of giving, working, sacrificing, discipline, and coordination of parts, is a model of success in both the individual athlete and in the athlete working with a team.

It is, in truth, the model of survival for the city, the state, and the nation.

The rebirth of the inner city, if it is to come about, will come about only from the spirit of the athlete, from the athlete in spirit. An athlete in spirit was a nearby chief executive, one who spent some of his teenage years at No. 61 Milford Avenue.

In his inaugural address on January 1, 1978, Edward I. Koch told the people of New York City that their task was not one of more money but of using money wisely; that they must give more than they ask and that a better city required "people who are willing to give of themselves, people who will fight for a cause . . ."

"We have been shaken by troubles that would have destroyed any other city," he said, "but we are the City of New York, and New York in adversity towers over any other city in the world."

In so stating, this athlete in spirit echoed not only the ancient Roman call for hard work and sacrifice, but also the athlete's creed of discipline, economy of effort, and smooth coordination of all parts for the good of the whole.

This then is the spirit of the athlete, the spirit that proclaims life, the spirit needed to rebuild the inner city.

It's a spirit that . . . who knows, maybe a spirit that probably would have broken down my mother's resistance to letting me and my "low resistance" go to Olympic Park on that long-ago summer day.

IRVING TAYLOR

Irv Taylor used to go to all the road races. He didn't start until he was forty-one years old, but he loved the competition, loved charging down the road full blast with a couple of dozen other devil-may-care characters and the people on the sidewalks turning to stare. He was one of the fastest runners his age, anywhere. At sixty-one he ran the Boston Marathon in 3:10. But he stopped racing in 1978, confining himself to solitary runs.

"Aaaah, a race is a race," he would mutter gruffly.

But you could hear a faint disappointment in his voice. I first heard him exclaim this in 1977, a year when running had obviously made the headlines, a far cry from the days in 1971 when I first met Irv at the races held in Newark's Branch Brook Park where he regularly competed. In his late fifties then, Irv more than held his own with much younger runners. With his bushy mustache and long wiry hair, you couldn't help notice him; there was a rough grace about him. Yet I knew little of him, and in all the races we made together, I never saw him arrive, never saw him leave, never knew how he got there or where he went afterward. It made no matter, though, for he was just there, part of the scene. That's how we took each other in those days

when there was an instant camaraderie among those of us who were, at the time, considered different.

But by 1977, things were rapidly changing. This was vividly portrayed in the setting of a thirteen-mile race through Westchester County. Though well organized and amply sponsored, it was so full of wall-to-wall runners that without a sophisticated buddy system, even before the event began, you were in danger of losing your companions forever.

In the race itself, I passed Irv at the eleven-mile mark. Though he was a superb competitor, Irving was not one ever to pace himself. It wasn't like him to learn some of the finer points. To him holding back meant putting out 95 percent the first half of a race and then compensating by giving it 105 percent the second half. So, despite his all-out efforts, he'd have to slow down a bit somewhere in the latter part of a race.

As I approached him, I first thought of just staying alongside of him, but this would be an act of running sacrilege. He'd know I was dogging it, and be deeply insulted. So, despite my ambivalence, I passed him and finished several minutes ahead of Irv. Once we met at the finish line after the race, I somehow felt sheepish and began to apologize for passing him, but he responded with a big bear hug, telling me that it was okay, that I must always, *always* remember, that "a race is a race."

Hearing Irv Taylor talk like that was a little bit like hearing the old New York Yankee catcher Yogi Berra saying, "The game isn't over till it's over." You kind of know what the guy means, but you don't expect too much elucidation. To ask for an explanation of an Irving-Taylorism is like asking Louis Armstrong to explain the meaning of jazz, to which he'd reply that if you need to have it explained, "You'll never know."

Still, the temptation to explain is irresistible. What comes to my mind is the intensity with which people— babies, college folks, and old men alike—go about the business of play. I think of the ball games we played as kids in the city streets, playing hard to win but forgetting the score immediately after it was over. We played in sandlots composed of stones and broken glass, in all types of weather. We played and we played and we played.

"To play," one could paraphrase Shakespeare, "is the thing." Johan Huizinga studied the elements of play, listing its special qualities, saying that it absorbed the player "intensely" and "utterly"; that nothing of material gain and profit can be derived from it; that it was done according to fixed rules, in an orderly manner, and within certain boundaries, promoting among its players social groupings stressing their differences from the common world. Carl Jung also recognized the need for play, with fantasy and imagination providing the building stones for later creative work. The early Greeks, too, were aware of our inherent need for play, and gave their god Eros dominion over both love and play.

Irv Taylor, more than anyone I know typifies Huizinga's attributes of "intensely" and "utterly." You can see it in that picture of him taken for the cover of a running booklet, published in 1974, called *Age of the Runner*. If you study his magnificently lined ascetic face, you see in his expression a look of fierce intensity. There are other runners, too, who are seen in the background, lined up facing at right angles to Irv. Irv's eyes have been momentarily diverted; his piercing glance has detected an intruder, the photographer, who has rudely invaded the boundaries of Irv's game. This was 1974, and in his face you can see an augury of things to come. Though no matinee idol, his strong weathered face belongs in an Ernest Hemingway movie, with a role usually played by Oscar Homolka or Gregory Ratoff, fighting bravely for a noble but hopeless cause.

By 1978 Irv's cause was a lonely one. He perceived elements in the running game that the rest of us had somehow either accepted or compromised with, but he was waging a battle verbally and by example. Earlier, Joe Henderson, too, must have seen something in Irv's look, for in 1974 Joe's words were prophetic:

> Today's newcomer might feel let down in 1979 when running isn't new to him anymore and is even more developed than now. He may look back on 1974 as his golden age.

It is October 1978, with four of us in a car going together to an eighteen-mile race. Irv tells us, in unambiguous phrases, of his thoughts on the golden age, an age that had now gone aglimmering down roads and streets beginning to show too many traces of Madison Avenue. "I'm at this race," he roared in short staccato bursts, "and here comes this fat guy with a $100 warm-up suit over to me, and he asks me how could he lose forty pounds and be like me. 'Look,' I told him, 'it took you all those years to put on those pounds. Keep them; don't be like me; you're happy with your weight. Don't bother me." He went on to rail against the faddists who'd never fathom the serious intensity of his play, against the exploiters who intensely fathomed only the serious business prospects of his play. He railed against the chic clothes (he liked his old sweatsuit and running shoes from the army-navy store); he railed against the garish ads in the slick magazines. He railed against all of them, the spoilsports, who had invaded and desecrated his hallowed ground. They were a disgrace, he said, "a dissgurrrrrase!"

Our homemade twentieth-century philosopher's lament was eloquently stated by the nineteenth-century philosopher William James, writing on the American mania for bigness:

> As for me, my bed is made: I am against big-ness and greatness in all their forms . . . The big-ger the unit you deal with, the hollower . . . So I am against all big organizations as such, na-tional ones first and foremost; against all big suc-cesses and big results; and in favor of the eternal forces of truth which always work in the indi-vidual and immediately unsuccessful way, under-dogs always, till history comes . . . and puts them on the top.

The years roll by and it's 1980. When you get to a certain age, if you saw someone a year ago, you say it's recent. But we had seen nothing of Irv, vaguely knew that he was still running but not racing, and that Sun-days were spent taking care of an ailing older sister. Two years were too long and we began to feel his absence. We missed him. So I called Irv during the Christmas holi-day season and he told me that yes, he was still running, but no more races. He couldn't tolerate the scene. It wasn't what it used to be. The closest he came to racing was watching the Jersey Marathon, and he didn't see anyone he knew. "Not one familiar face, we used to be like a family, no more though."

No, he didn't have the 1974 *New York Times* article written about him. Furthermore, he gave his daughter all the clippings and medals. They were mementos of days that were "fun and enjoyable," but the trophies, medals, and newspaper notices were "unimportant." But yes, he would like to run with us and see the guys again, and we made a tentative date the second Sunday in January to run together.

I called him two weeks later to confirm the date, but he couldn't make it; "a family tragedy," he explained. His niece had slipped on an icy surface and broken her arm, had shattered it so badly that they were considering amputation. Tomorrow he would be taking his sister to the hospital in Connecticut. He talked on, how the week before the family was together, talking, joking, laughing, and now this. He couldn't sleep all last night, and he couldn't get the whole thing off his mind. As the conversation faltered, I mumbled the usual awkward, helpless phrases, and made him promise to keep in touch. I thought he said good-bye, but as I was hanging up the phone, I heard him still talking.

"What's that, Irv?" I asked.

"Thanks," he said, "for listening."

How ironic it is that this unique man will somehow inspire the most hackneyed expressions. I am tempted to say, "way back when," and "the good old days," yet if the truth be told, we were always taking about the good old days when we were in the midst of what were supposed to be the "good old days." I am so tempted to call him "the last of the . . ." something or other that I have dubbed him "the last angry runner," a variation on Gerald Green's theme in *The Last Angry Man*, the novel of a doctor, like Irv, a noble anachronism, who was quoting Thoreau and growing corn in the backyard of his house, which sat amid the poverty and squalor of the decaying Brooklyn neighborhood where he practiced. Here was a man who would entertain company by serving homemade ice cream sodas instead of cocktails, a man who spoke out against the quacks, against the "galoots," against those conscienceless drug companies who were concerned only for profit.

But while angry runners and angry doctors await history's vindication, time, snugly encased within countless pairs of Pumas, Nikes, and Tigers, moves inexorably on. Progress is inevitable. No one can push back the digital clock. Besides, you can make the argument that on balance we are better off: Races are on schedule; we have computer printouts; we are noticed by everybody; the water stations are well manned; and from the lettering on our T-shirts, we learn the names of many products and businesses.

But if we runners ever had our shining moment, our "fleeting wisp of glory," our Camelot, it was the early 1970s, a simpler, more innocent time for running, a time when you'd get a mailed race application two weeks after the race was held, when after a race you'd crowd around a guy with a stopwatch, or get your results in the boiler room of a Branch Brook Park "clubhouse," where on one occasion everyone got a medal because there were more awards than there were participants. It was a time when the running movement, seeking that elusive thing called truth, would come across the path Irv had been running on for many years, and stay with him for a while because he was a vital nutritive element in the running blend.

Yet like Camelot, it was only a brief moment, for when there were thrown into the mixture too many impure ingredients and artificial additives, there was nothing for an Irving Taylor to do but excuse himself from the training table upon which they were serving a running stew he could not swallow.

How I miss the good old days, yes, good old days, days when we knew one another and no one knew us, days when it was all play and no profit, days when there was an Irving Taylor to remind us that . . . "a race is a race."

JOAN BENOIT AND HER DOG

Hardly noticed on ABC's *Up Close and Personal*—shown just minutes before the 1984 first-ever women's Olympic marathon actually began—was Joan Benoit's running companion, a Labrador retriever puppy. While the background voice of Jim McKay was telling of Maine, ". . . the real Maine, rock-ribbed and unyielding, with wild waves and quiet woods and time to be alone," Joan Benoit was running alone with her dog.

(Are you starting to smile a little? You are, aren't you? We often do smile, begin to chuckle, even giggle when we talk about animals. Especially dogs.)

I once had two grown Labrador retrievers: Barney, a yellow-coated 100-pounder, and Quasi, a black and slightly smaller version. The breed comes in chocolate shade, too; all have the characteristic narrow alert eyes, set back in a broad noble head supported by a thick muscular neck sitting on wide sloping shoulders that frame a deep barrel chest.

Usually docile inside the house, the dogs begin to wag their tails furiously and become suddenly importunate at any hint—the baggy red sweatpants and oversized sweatshirt I've changed into usually does it—that we're going across the street into the woods. If I tarry

too long, I do so at my own peril. So I make haste to finish donning my running apparel.

We cross the macadam road to reach the other side. Paralleling the road and rimming the long miles of vegetation are the many traces of human visitation: the assorted beer cans, soda bottles, discarded cardboard cartons with their red and black labels. But once inside the semi-penetrable wall of tall maples, oaks, and pines, we are walled off from the mundane world. We are inside New Jersey's Watchung Reservations, our small version of the "Real Maine."

Down one of the winding trails the dogs bound ahead of me, stopping to sniff out the many scents, or to stake out their territorial claims in short watery spurts. We soon come across one of the many serpentine streambeds, footprints of a receding glacial age. One of these streams leads to Surprise Lake where the trail widens and the reddish yellow-brown October leaves underfoot give us a soft carpet to journey on.

Barney and Quasi will now go into their ritual and habitual atavistic routine, stopping at an imaginary starting line, then race, actually race. After a hundred yards or so, they abruptly break off their contest at some arbitrary point and continue on again, though with less apparent direction.

The three of us now romp along together and re-enact in miniature an ancient pantomime played out thousands of years before, where man and dog daily trekked and ran long miles together in quest of food and shelter. Those were the times when sheer survival depended on raw stamina and particularly the ability to run long distances, where man's canine counterpart would corner an animal often larger than he, then wait until his master came for the kill. In more recent times, the Labrador would be used to plunge into icy waters

Barney

to fetch the fallen prey.

Feet and paws beat a slow rhythmic tattoo upon the thick leaves that have covered what was earlier in the season exposed roots and hard ground. The dogs' attentions are diverted by the traces and spoor of other forest creatures, but soon they rejoin me, and Barney jumps at my side signaling that he wants me to throw a stick. With little break in stride I pick up a dead branch and throw it diagonally in front of him into the lake, where this hardy descendant of Newfoundland's Arctic climes dives with a wild grace. We repeat this a few more times as he retrieves the branch, then splashes back into the water swimming in a straight line toward the prized object floating a chip-shot away in the middle of the lake. They will dive into the same lake, with the same abandon, months from now when the ice has barely melted and the land is still enveloped in a smooth blanket of white. It is just this combination of hardiness, stamina, good nature, and keen intelligence that makes the Labrador a choice pupil to train for, and an ideal companion of, blind people. (I must admit, however, that Barney and Quasi were both "adopted" by us when they flunked out of the Seeing Eye Training School.)

If our canine friends were our ancestors' comrades in ancient times when a twenty-six-mile marathon run of today would be like an early-morning stroll then, then too the dog was rather more their teacher in an older, even more innate, activity we renew on any run. That activity is of play itself. "Play," wrote Johan Huizinga in his classic monograph *Homo Ludens* (Man the Player), "is older than culture . . . and animals have not waited for man to teach them their playing."

Awareness of our inherent need to play is evident as far back as Greco-Roman times when the god Eros was assigned dominion not only over love, but also over play, indicating the ancient intuitive appreciation of the intertwining of these two needs. And Eros was always depicted as a child. Children and dogs come naturally to the art of play.

"Animals play just like men," Huizinga continues. "We have only to watch young dogs to see that all the essentials of human play are present in their merry gambols, [and] in all these things they plainly experience tremendous fun and enjoyment."

Huizinga also pointed out that play absorbed the

player "utterly" and "intensely." So it is with the dog. He is intense in his play, playful in his intensity. In play he is not only our friend, but also our model. Is it then his playful intensity, reminding us of the child within, that always makes us smile, or chuckle, or giggle?

About two and half hours after the ABC *Personal*, Joan Benoit was beginning to absorb the impact of what she had just accomplished. Speaking into the ABC microphone, she told the world that her victory had been possible only because of all the special people who had helped her along the way. In giving her thanks to them, I have a hunch she also included her dog. You could tell. She had that little smile.

SWIM FOR RICHARD

Here are the dry land, dry facts: Three of us had entered a relay team to swim the twenty-four miles of Tampa Bay. We made this into a fund-raiser to bring more public awareness to bipolar disorder. Funds raised were targeted for both research into the malady and for "Strong Kids," an arm of the local YMCA sending kids to summer day camp, where they spend much of their days in playful physical activities.

The two causes complement each other since there is convincing evidence that strong body equals strong mind.

A year ago, a tragedy befell the family of one of us, suicide, a by-product of the son's bipolar disorder. There is some indication, however, that exercise, in the right amounts, has a beneficial effect on bipolar and related depressive disorders. Well-run scientific studies indicate that exercise, be it swimming, running, skiing, kayaking, or biking, done regularly, has a positive effect on modifying, preventing, and treating the major depression states.

Bipolar disorder is, however, tricky, with a high suicide potential. More research is needed. With our relay team comrade, genetics appeared to be a strong element. Martino's father and now his son, Richard, were suicides. Accordingly, money raised will have been donated to a nonprofit research organization investigating the role of genes in bipolar disorder.

Martino composed the words in an imagined letter to his departed son, Richard. With his words and Doug's photos, come with us now on our swim journey.

Dearest Richard,

It will soon be a year since you took leave from this world. The void left in our life from your departure makes us realize what an incredible blessing your life has been to us all.

It is still dark as Doug, Paul and myself are getting ready to start the 24-mile swim in your memory: a handful of swimmers of all ages and from all places on the beach begin, at 7A.M., a long journey from the St. Petersburg marina to the finishing line in Tampa.

I am chosen to be the first one to swim for our relay: the water is at about 68 degrees, warmer than the air temperature, tears are streaming down my face as I start swimming and a mixture of grief, sorrow, gratitude,

and emotion take over; I thank you for helping me getting here and making this happen and I swim.

Right now, in the cold water and in the dark, I am not so sure that the 3 Y's guys are wise after all, but we are certainly proud to be trying to accomplish this and excited about the adventure ahead of us.

The kayaker, a young student of marine biology, does an excellent job of directing our swim as we try to take advantage of tides and currents and avoid having to swim against high tide, due to come later in the afternoon.

He reassured us somewhat telling us that sharks are indeed coming to the bay, but only later in the year and only to mate: quite right but what if a shark has sexual needs that manifest themselves out of season?

I only hope that he is a good student of marine biology and start to swim quite fast, just in case . . .

The captain of our support boat confirms the theory: He has seen quite a few sharks in his twenty years of diving in the bay, but was never bothered. Yes, sure, but what if the shark is attracted by Italian food?

Boat captain and kayaker are integral part of the team and play a fundamental role in the swim as they help the swimmer minimizing zigzagging and avoiding currents and tides that have proven to be the main reason for swimmers not being able to complete these long swims.

Doug follows in the water as the second swimmer: His swim looks smooth and effective as a couple of dolphins swim for a short while alongside him.

Paul has been working the whole 80 minutes he is on the boat, waiting to get into the water, to get rid of the layers of clothing he is wearing, trying to keep himself warm in the cool morning temperature and putting on the fancy swimwear he has chosen for this effort, which includes a thermal swim-cap that makes him look like a Russian cosmonaut of Cold War time.

It is now Paul's turn, the sun is out and we all welcome the rise in air temperature: It helps feeling the warm sunrays on your back as you swim in cold water, and it is nice to bask in the sun on the boat as you wait for your turn to swim.

Paul's swim looks very relaxed and easy: I continue to be amazed by the fact that this young man of 79 has been instrumental in getting us here to do this!

Doug and Paul, two scientists, have put together a nutrition plan for the day based on fruit, power bars, and a patented concoction that has the great advantage of looking disgusting enough to make you want to be back in the water rather than having to swallow the stuff.

The Italian in me makes me stick to real food and I enjoy my roast-beef sandwich and fruit salad as I complain with the captain for not having on board an espresso machine!

Starbucks is a step in the right direction but complete civilization is still a long way to go.

Seagulls, pelicans, and all kind of birds fly low to the water, probably attracted by the shining silver cap worn by Doug, thinking that it might be the back of a large fish, but they do not dive for it, so we do not mention it to him and let him go on with his swim.

Water is alternately shallow and deep, warmer and

cooler: The swimmers on the boat make a great amount of calculations estimating the distance covered and the time elapsed and assessing the probability of being able to finish the swim before sunset, the time limit accepted for finishing.

We approach the first major landmark, a bridge at about 18 miles from the start: This is when we feel that we can make it and when the mood begins to become optimistic about the outcome of our effort.

As we begin to see the finishing spot, we agree that we would swim the final few hundred yards together and get out of the water as a team: Doug is now at the end of his sixth forty-minute swim as Paul and I jump in the shallow water and a young man standing on a surfing board paddles alongside us to make sure that the jet skiers stay away from us.

Quite a surreal painting: three mature man led by a very young surfer to the beach in water so shallow that it is harder to swim than to it is to walk.

The emotion however is now for me extreme, I struggle to swim as I am sobbing in the water, all the

pent-up feelings are now surfacing and they are way stronger than any current or tide can ever be: As we get out of the water and walk onto the beach people are cheering, leaning over the restaurant balcony by the finishing line, applauding, I am totally overwhelmed as I hug Mom and we both cry and sob in each other arms.

Eleven hours and 19 minutes of swimming behind us, we are overwhelmed by the reception and by the outpour of support from the crowd surrounding us: They are all cheering for you, Ritchie, and for all the people who suffer as you have and for their families!

Thank you Richard for being with me all the way, I would not have been able to do it without your help: I am somewhat comforted by the thought that you are now at peace and that the illness that has taken you away from us is not tormenting you anymore.

Now, we are carrying on your battle against it for you and we hope that also thanks to our little, infinitesimal contribution, other people might one day be spared the terrifying, devastating experience we have gone through.

Ciao Richard, I love you now more than ever and miss you terribly, rest in peace my boy, one day we will be together again, this time forever.

Dad

CONCLUSIONS

Writing in *The Republic* about twenty-five hundred years ago, Plato recommended that every school have a gymnasium and a playground where sport and play would constitute the entire curriculum; at least for the first ten years of life education should be mostly physical. This way, he opined, enough health would then be generated and stored to make all medicine unnecessary.

Philosopher, physician, and psychologist William James put it well:

"Keep the faculty of effort alive in you by a little bit of gratuitous exercise every day . . . so that when the hour of dire need draws nigh, it may find you not unnerved and untrained to stand the test" (*The Principles of Psychology*, 1890).

Fast forwarding to the present, perhaps the words of Dr. Jeremy Morris sum up this whole process. "Exercise," that grand man wrote, "normalizes the workings of the body."

Consider exercise a stress, an irritant, the challenge that stimulates a physical response to the mild injury it causes when a boundary becomes trespassed, such as a membrane, a lining, a tendon, or a muscle. Done in measured dosages, by virtue of the over-reaction of the body, we become stronger. The words of the philosopher Friedrich Nietzsche are apt: "What does not kill me, makes me stronger" (*Twilight of the Idols*).

Two analogies come to mind:

One is the response of the body to the germs that may invade our membranes and tissues. This invasion sets off an alarm. Once sounded the cavalry, in the form of white blood cells, come to engulf and destroy the offending organism. The body then becomes attuned to further onslaught by the same offending agent, and in this sense, becomes stronger. Such describes the immunization procedure.

Best of all, take a look at the dealings between the oyster and its sand irritant-stressor, their interaction giving birth to the precious pearl. Exercise in the right dose is the medicine that brings about vital and precious transformations. It is a force uniting body, mind, and spirit.

GLOSSARY OF TERMS

This is to afford a working understanding of scientific terms commonly encountered, either in this work or in any of the references the reader may consult.

ACTH: A protein hormone of the anterior lobe of the pituitary gland that stimulates the adrenal cortex—called also adrenocorticotrophic hormone.

Addiction: Compulsive need for and use of a habit-forming substance (as heroin, nicotine, or alcohol) characterized by tolerance and by well-defined physiological symptoms upon withdrawal.

Aerobic Exercise: *Aerobic* literally means "with oxygen." It refers to exercise sufficiently strenuous to create an increased demand for oxygen, increasing, in turn, the heartbeat and breathing. Exercise, however, that is aerobic means there is a balance, a "steady state" between supply and demand of oxygen and nutrients to the exercising muscles.

Anaerobic Exercise: Exercise strenuous enough so that the demand for oxygen and nutrients to the exercising muscles is not met and an oxygen "debt" is created leading to build up of lactic acid and a slowing down and inefficiency in performing a particular activity.

Anxiety: An abnormal and overwhelming sense of apprehension and fear often marked by physiological signs (as sweating, tension, and increased pulse), by doubt concerning the reality and nature of the threat, and by self-doubt about one's capacity to cope with it, particularly when the source of the fear is not apparent.

Autonomic nervous system: That part of the vertebrate nervous system that enervates smooth muscle (the organs) and cardiac muscle and glandular tissues, and governs involuntary actions (as secretion, vasoconstriction, or peristalsis). It consists of the sympathetic nervous system and the parasympathetic nervous system.

Beta-Endorphin: An endorphin of the pituitary gland with much greater analgesic potency than morphine.

Blood-Brain Barrier: The walls of the blood vessels and capillaries of the central nervous system are thought to be thicker and more selective, keeping certain materials in the blood from reaching the tissue and cells of the central nervous system.

Central Nervous System (CNS): Refers to the brain and the spinal cord.

Cerebrospinal Fluid (CSF): A fluid distillate flowing in the canal within the spinal cord that continues into the brain, where it widens and forms the ventricles.

Cognitive: Refers to the mental processes of comprehending, judging, memorizing, reasoning.

Control Group: Scores/results on any experiment are compared in one group not receiving the treatment, for example, to the same scores in the experimental (treatment) group, to counter the possibility that the experimental results could have otherwise come about spontaneously, over time, and without the experimental process (treatment). Control groups should be matched with the experimental group for age, gender, and other relevant characteristics.

Defense Mechanisms: Automatic unconscious intrapsychic processes serving to provide relief from emotional conflict and anxiety and to maintain self-esteem, including repression, denial, rationalization, displacement, overcompensation, dissociation, sublimation, and reaction formation.

Double Blind: A study where one or more administered drugs and a placebo are compared without doctor or patient knowing which preparation is being administered.

Dysphoria: A disorder of mood. A state of feeling unwell or unhappy.

Electrocardiogram (ECG or EKG): A graphic tracing of the electric current produced by the contraction of the heart muscle.

Endogenous: Caused by factors within the body or mind or arising from internal structural or functional causes.

Endorphinergic: Pertaining to endorphin-like activity.

Endorphin: One of the body's own naturally manufactured morphine-like substances.

Exogenous: Arising from an exernal source.

Ganglia: Refers to localized pockets/aggregations of nerve cells.

Hatha Yoga: Involves a gentle form of stretching, balancing, and breathing routines. Both the Hatha Yoga and swimming facilitate abdominal breathing.

Hemodynamic: Pertaining to the movements involved in the circulation of the blood.

Hippocampus: A curved elongated ridge that is an important part of the cerebrum, extends over the floor of the descending horn of each lateral ventricle of the brain, and consists of gray matter covered on the ventricular surface with white matter. The hippocampus is involved with the function of memory.

Homeostasis: The maintenance of relatively stable internal physiological conditions (such as body temperature or the pH of blood) under fluctuating environmental conditions.

Limbic System: Thought to be the area of the brain that controls emotion, it begins in sections (lobes) of the cerebral cortex with connections to other parts of the brain.

Mental Mechanisms: A generic term for certain processes that are functions of the ego such as memory and perception, as well as defense mechanisms.

Meta-analysis: This refers to studies made at different locales or with different experimental groups examining the same thing, using similar methods, which are then combined and compared.

Metabolism: The sum total of all the physical and chemical processes by which living tissue is both produced and maintained.

Mood: A conscious state of mind or predominant emotion.

Naloxone: Generic name of a substance that counteracts the action of a narcotic, such as morphine.

Neuron(e): A nerve cell.

Opiate: Preparation or derivative of opium.

Opioid: Having characteristics of an opiate.

Organic: When this term is used it can variously relate to either a bodily organ, to living things, or to anything containing carbon or its compounds.

Peripheral Nervous System: Nerves and nerve cells outside of the membranes (coverings) of the brain and spinal cord.

Physiology: The science that studies the functions of living organisms and their constituent parts.

Pituitary Gland: The "master" gland, located in the brain, which regulates the other glands in the body, such as via thyroid-stimulating hormone or ACTH.

Psyche: Refers to the mind.

Radio-immunoassay: Measurement of tagged radioactive antibodies produced in animals by the introduction of whatever substance is being studied, endorphins.

Random assignment: When a group of experimental subjects are chosen from a larger group, each of whose members has an equal probability of being chosen for the experimental group.

Receptor: The portion of a cell that has the function of attaching to or combining with, a particular circulating substance.

Stress: Any challenge or stimulus, physical or mental, calling for a response. *Stress* is an overused misunderstood term. Stress is healthy when it is a stimulus for successful response and therefore a strengthening or maturing. But if the ability to cope with the challenge is inadequate and fails, the result is distress.

Type A Personality: A description of a type of person who is constantly striving, has a need to achieve, is frequently racing the clock, is impatient and unable to wait. At first thought to have a strong relationship to heart disease, its correlation has been found to be less significant than initially thought. When, however, the personality is associated with high levels of hostility, particularly accrued when thwarted or unappreciated, it is the hostility that makes for a strong correlation with heart disease if such coexists in the personality type.

VO_2 max: A measure of the maximum volume of oxygen that the blood can deliver to the working muscles.

Yoga: A system of exercises for attaining bodily or mental control and well-being.